THE OFFICIAL
HAMMERS
2018/19 YEARBOOK

Contributors: Peter Rogers & Rob Mason

A TWOCAN PUBLICATION

©2018. Published by twocan under licence from West Ham United FC.

ISBN: 978-1-912692-26-2

PICTURE CREDITS: Action Images, Getty Images, Griffiths Photographers, Press Association.

2018

AUGUST 2018

Sunday	12	Liverpool	A	
Saturday	18	**Bournemouth**	H	
Saturday	25	Arsenal	A	
Tuesday	28	AFC Wimbledon	A	EFL Cup 2

SEPTEMBER 2018

Saturday	01	**Wolves**	H	
Sunday	16	Everton	A	
Sunday	23	**Chelsea**	H	
Wednesday	26	**Macclesfield Town**	H	EFL Cup 3
Saturday	29	**Manchester United**	H	

OCTOBER 2018

Friday	05	Brighton & HA	A	
Saturday	20	**Tottenham Hotspur**	H	
Saturday	27	Leicester City	A	
Wednesday	31	**Tottenham Hotspur**	H	EFL Cup 4

NOVEMBER 2018

Saturday	03	**Burnley**	H	
Saturday	10	Huddersfield Town	A	
Saturday	24	**Manchester City**	H	

DECEMBER 2018

Saturday	01	Newcastle United	A	
Tuesday	04	**Cardiff City**	H	
Saturday	08	**Crystal Palace**	H	
Saturday	15	Fulham	A	
Wednesday	19			EFL Cup 5
Saturday	22	**Watford**	H	
Thursday	27	Southampton	A	
Sunday	30	Burnley	A	

PREMIER LEAGUE
FIXTURES

2019

WEST HAM UNITED LONDON

JANUARY 2019

Wednesday	**02**	**Brighton & HA**	**H**	
Saturday	05			FA Cup 3
Wednesday	09			EFL Cup SF1
Saturday	**12**	**Arsenal**	**H**	
Saturday	19	Bournemouth	A	
Wednesday	23			EFL Cup SF2
Saturday	26			FA Cup 4
Tuesday	29	Wolves	A	

FEBRUARY 2019

Saturday	**02**	**Liverpool**	**H**	
Saturday	09	Crystal Palace	A	
Saturday	16			FA Cup 5
Saturday	**23**	**Fulham**	**H**	
Sunday	24			EFL Cup Final
Wednesday	27	Manchester City	A	

MARCH 2019

Saturday	**02**	**Newcastle United**	**H**	
Saturday	09	Cardiff City	A	
Saturday	**16**	**Huddersfield Town**	**H**	FA Cup 6
Saturday	**30**	**Everton**	**H**	

APRIL 2019

Saturday	06	Chelsea	A	FA Cup SF
Saturday	13	Manchester United	A	
Saturday	**20**	**Leicester City**	**H**	
Saturday	27	Tottenham Hotspur	A	

MAY 2019

Saturday	**04**	**Southampton**	**H**	
Sunday	12	Watford	A	
Saturday	18			FA Cup Final

TED 2018/2019

TOP (L TO R): Hugo Scheckter (Head of Player Care), Conor Coventry, Josh Cullen, Manuel Lanzini, Angelo Ogbonna, Andy Carroll, Issa Diop, Andriy Yarmolenko, Fabian Balbuena, Declan Rice, Reece Oxford, Nathan Holland, James Saban (Kit Manager)

MIDDLE (L TO R): Richard Collinge (Head of Medical), Jamie Osman (Head of Performance Analysis), Xavi Valero (Goalkeeper Coach), Carlos Sanchez, Robert Snodgrass, Ryan Fredericks, Adrian, Lukasz Fabianski, Nathan Trott, Winston Reid, Pedro Obiang, Michail Antonio, Lucas Perez, Jose Cabello (Fitness Coach), Felix Cao (Assistant Fitness Coach), Mario Husillos (Director of Football)

FRONT (L TO R): Aaron Cresswell, Felipe Anderson, Arthur Masuaku, Mark Noble, Ruben Cousillas (Assistant Coach), Manuel Pellegrini, Enzo Maresca (Second Assistant Coach), Pablo Zabaleta, Marko Arnautovic, Chicharito, Jack Wilshere

9

HAMMER OF THE YEAR

MARKO
ARNAUTOVIC

With an overwhelming 68 per cent of the vote, Marko Arnautovic marked his first season at the club by becoming the 2017/18 Hammer of the Year.

Signed from Stoke City for a club record £25m, the Austria international proved to be well worth the investment with eleven goals and four assists in his 31 appearances.

"I am very happy and very proud" said a beaming Arnautovic, adding, "I want to thank every single fan who supports West Ham for this award. It means a lot to me. It was hard for me at the beginning of the season, but now it's going well and I want to do my job for many years to come. We are not finished yet."

Finishing was something that Marko got better and better at, the longer the season went on. A first goal on his twelfth appearance was worth waiting for as he delighted the London Stadium faithful with the only goal of the game to defeat Chelsea in December.

A week later, Arnautovic was 'on the Marko' back at his old stomping ground at Stoke where the Irons triumphed 3-0. It proved to be a happy Christmas with another three goals in his next two games, at home to Newcastle United followed by a Boxing Day brace at Bournemouth.

Further goals in wins at Huddersfield and at home to Watford preceded another brace in a 3-0 victory over Southampton, a strike at Arsenal and finally the last goal of the campaign to seal a 3-1 home win over Everton.

As vital as they were, Marko's goals were just part of his Hammer of the Year story. His power, quick-feet and ability to play on the edge, make him a player opponents fear and West Ham fans want to see given the ball. Emphatic finishes, impudent skill and sheer quality come together to make Arnautovic a fitting name to add to the legends that adorn the Hammer of the Year roll of honour.

Marko became the 40th different recipient of the coveted Hammer of the Year award, with second and third places going to Declan Rice and Pablo Zabaleta. The Hammer of the Year accolade capped a stunning hat-trick for Arnautovic on awards evening as he also collected the prizes for Signing of the Season and Players' Player of the Season.

West Ham United played seven warm-up matches ahead of their 2018/19 Premier League campaign, with new boss Manuel Pellegrini introducing new signings and his own ideas to the squad throughout July and August in preparation for the season ahead.

2018/19 PRE-SEASON PREPARATIONS

A busy pre-season programme saw the Hammers face a number of different types of opposition as Pellegrini worked on fitness and team play while also introducing the players to his plans and ideas for the forthcoming campaign.

In the main, the pre-season matches provided an impressive array of results with just one defeat and the winning of the Betway Cup following a dramatic penalty shoot-out success in Austria.

It all began when Pellegrini and his newly-inherited squad headed out to Bad Ragaz in Switzerland for an intensive training camp in early July. At the end of their first week's training, the Hammers took on Swiss Challenge League side FC Winterthur on Sunday 8 July.

The new boss managed to cast his eye across 22 players, with one side playing the first-half, before an alternative team played the second period. Andy Carroll and Mark Noble were both on target for the Hammers, who got valuable match minutes into their legs on a hot and sunny afternoon at the Stadion Schutzenwiese. However, it was the home side that ran out 3-2 winners.

Once the squad had returned to the UK, their next assignment was a short trip to face League One new boys Wycombe Wanderers at Adams Park on Saturday 14 July.

Marko Arnautovic scored the only goal of the game firing into the far corner with 34 minutes on the clock – and the Austrian's goal on his first appearance of the summer proved enough to settle the contest.

Along with debutant Andriy Yarmolenko, Arnautovic provided a serious threat in the opening period. As changes were made throughout the second half, the pace of the game dropped, but the Hammers came through a good workout with a first win of pre-season ahead of their next match away to Championship side Preston North End.

Arnautovic continued his scoring form netting twice and Jack Wilshere made an impressive debut following his arrival from Arsenal, as Pellegrini's men drew 2-2 with Alex Neil's Preston on Saturday 21 July.

Just as he had been at Wycombe Wanderers the previous weekend, Arnautovic was on target, netting two well-taken first half goals at Deepdale.

Alongside Arnautovic, debutant Wilshere also caught the eye, winning the free-kick which led to the Austrian's seventh-minute opener and driving his team forward at every opportunity.

Ukraine star Yarmolenko also followed up his own impressive debut with another eye-catching display in Lancashire, capped by an assist for Arnautovic's second goal on the stroke of half-time.

In between Arnautovic's two strikes, Preston had levelled through captain Tom Clarke's powerful header, and the hosts grabbed a share of the spoils through substitute Billy Bodin's smart control and finish with 15 minutes remaining.

A busy week of fixtures against Championship opposition continued on Wednesday 25 July as the Hammers faced Aston Villa at Walsall's Banks's Stadium. Michail Antonio and Marko Arnautovic scored in the first half, before a late goal from Robert Snodgrass secured a 3-1 pre-season victory.

Antonio put the Irons in front inside ten minutes with a low effort, having fashioned the opportunity himself, before Arnautovic netted his fourth goal in three matches following a fantastic team move.

The match also saw West Ham debuts for record-signing Felipe Anderson and defender Fabian Balbuena, with the duo both impressing on their first showings for the side.

Substitute Snodgrass, playing against the club he spent the majority of 2017/18 on loan with, put the game to bed with five minutes to go. The Scottish international rounded 'keeper Jed Steer and slotted home the Hammers' third goal of the evening, before Andre Green powered home a strike for Villa in the dying embers of the game.

The trio of Championship challenges was concluded with a trip to Portman Road to face Ipswich Town on Saturday 28 July. Backed by over 4,000 travelling fans, the Hammers continued the fine work they produced against Villa in midweek with another winning performance in the Suffolk sunshine.

Anderson scored his first goal in Claret and Blue and Arnautovic was on target yet again as West Ham ran out 2-1 winners.

Having dominated against Villa last time out, West Ham were given a sterner test by Paul Hurst's team, who could have snatched a draw on another day.

Pellegrini's side were ahead within three minutes through the unlikely source of Anderson's forehead. Picking up from where they left off in midweek, just 145 seconds had elapsed when three of West Ham's summer signings combined to give their new team the lead.

Yarmolenko's threaded through ball sent Ryan Fredericks clear into space behind Ipswich left-back Jonas Knudsen and, when he crossed at head height, the Brazil winger had stolen a yard on former Hammer Jordan Spence and nodded inside the far post.

There was little goalmouth action until Ipswich equalised nine minutes later when striker Ellis Harrison poked a first-time shot past debutant Lukasz Fabianski in the West Ham goal.

The second half saw Snodgrass test Bartosz Bialkowski with a powerful low drive before Pellegrini's side grabbed the victory with a goal that owed almost everything to Arnautovic.

The Austrian showed power and pace to race away from the Ipswich centre-halves and latch on to substitute Sead Haksabanovic's through pass and poke nonchalantly past Bialkowski and into the corner to score his fifth goal in five pre-season appearances.

With both managers making a succession of substitutions, the game lost its flow, but Fabianski was called upon to make a smart save from Dozzell that ensured he would end his debut on the winning side.

West Ham United finally secured the Betway Cup with a dramatic penalty shootout victory over FSV Mainz in Austria on the final day of July.

The Hammers looked on course to win the trophy in normal time when substitute Toni Martinez headed his side ahead midway through the second half.

However, a deflected equaliser from the German Bundesliga side's Robin Quaison eight minutes from the end sent the match straight to penalties.

Adrian saved one spot-kick and scored another, before Gaetan Bussman skied his effort high and wide of the Spaniard's goal to make it fourth time lucky for the men in Claret and Blue, who had previously been beaten by Werder Bremen (twice) and Juventus in the pre-season competition sponsored by the club's principal partner.

The Hammers wrapped up their pre-season preparations on Friday 3 August when Chicharito marked his return to the team with the winning goal in a 1-0 victory over Angers SCO in Austria.

The Hammers edged past their French Ligue 1 opponents with a goal from the Mexico star midway through the first half at the Das.Goldberg Stadion in Grodig.

15

GOAL OF THE YEAR

PEDRO
OBIANG

TOTTENHAM HOTSPUR 1
WEST HAM UNITED 1

PREMIER LEAGUE · 4 JANUARY 2018

Pedro Obiang was so far out when he lined up his shot against Spurs, that he might as well have been at White Hart Lane rather than Wembley Stadium. Celebrations for the New Year were still fresh in the mind. Forty eight hours earlier, a brace from Andy Carroll had helped the Hammers come from behind to start 2018 with a home win over West Bromwich Albion.

Spurs were full of confidence, coming into the match on the back of three successive wins and having slotted five past Swansea in their most recent home fixture. What proved to be a hard-fought game, was on a knife-edge as both teams probed for a break-through three-quarters of the way through the contest.

West Ham's quality led to the breakthrough. After long periods of determined defending, patient controlled possession down the left flank saw Manuel Lanzini and Arthur Masuaku combine to bring Pedro Obiang into play. At this point in the game West Ham had not had a shot on goal, while Tottenham boasted 20. Picking the ball up some 40 yards out, Obiang looked around, but had no options, so took the responsibility on his own shoulders.

Striding forward the former Spain U21 international struck a shot of fearsome velocity into the top corner. Home goalkeeper Hugo Lloris will have looked forward to seeing the goal on the TV highlights so he could see the shot for himself, because he can barely have witnessed Obiang's strike.

It was a goal worthy of winning any game and until the closing stages, it looked as if it would win this one despite the home side being on top. The Irons showed enormous determination to hold Tottenham at bay, despite Spurs piling on the pressure. Over the 90 minutes The Lilywhites had 31 attempts to the three West Ham managed under David Moyes. The players gave it their all, blocking 13 shots while Adrian made seven saves. Indeed, Adrian celebrated Obiang's wonder-strike as if he had scored it himself and deserved a clean sheet only for Spurs' South Korean striker Heung-Min Son to finally beat him with a quality goal of his own with just seven minutes remaining.

"We have scored a goal and so have they - they can have as many shots as they like" said a satisfied David Moyes who added, "It was a great finish from Obiang, unexpected. He struck it brilliantly well."

At the 61st West Ham United Player Awards, a glittering evening in association with Betway at the Intercontinental London- the 02 Hotel was hosted by Gabby Logan and Alvin Martin. Pedro was a popular and deserving winner of The Goal of the Year award and when the time comes to assess the Goal of the Decade Obiang's heat-seeker must be in the running.

LUKASZ
FABIANSKI

SQUAD NO:	**1**
POSITION:	Goalkeeper
DoB:	18 April 1985
BIRTHPLACE:	Kostrzyn nad Odr

Poland international Fabianski signed for West Ham United for a reported £7m fee on a three-year contract in the summer of 2018.

Most recently with Swansea City, as a boy Lukasz started with Polonia Slubice before progressing with MSP Szamotuly. He first came to prominence with Lech Poznan followed by a couple of seasons with Legia Warsaw where he competed with present-day Bournemouth 'keeper Artur Boruc, who he has also competed with at international level for much of his career.

Fabianski came to England in 2007, joining Arsenal who paid a reported £2.1m for his signature. In his seven-year stint with the Gunners, he made 78 appearances including 32 in the Premier League, while cup experience included playing in the Champions League and winning the FA Cup.

Moving to Swansea for regular first-team football, Fabianski never missed more than one Premier League game per year in four seasons with the Swans where he was Player of the Year in 2017/18 prior to playing in the summer's World Cup finals.

THE SQUAD 2018/19

WEST HAM UNITED LONDON

SQUAD NO	**2**
POSITION:	Defender
DoB:	3 July 1988
BIRTHPLACE:	North Shore, Auckland, New Zealand

Born in New Zealand, Winston moved to Denmark when he was ten years old and came through the ranks of FC Midtjylland after initially being connected to a club called SUB Sonderborg.

Although he represented the Danes at U19, U20 and U21 levels, it was with the nation of his birth that he became a full international, playing, and even scoring, in the 2010 FIFA World Cup finals.

Reid was only 17 when he made his league debut in Denmark, going on to play just short of 100 games before being signed by West Ham in August 2010. Hammer of the Year in his third season at the club in 2012/13, the following year brought an international accolade as New Zealand Player of the Year.

A knee operation was scheduled to rule Winston out of the opening three months of the 2018/19 season, but once Reid returns, his availability will undoubtedly strengthen the Irons.

WINSTON REID

19

AARON CRESSWELL

Hammer of the Year as well as Players' Player of the Year in his first season at the club in 2014/15, Cresswell's quality has subsequently seen him go on to collect full England honours.

Liverpool-born, Aaron began his career with Tranmere Rovers debuting in November 2008 in a League One fixture with MK Dons. After 80 games for Rovers, Aaron switched to Ipswich Town in 2011, missing only six league games in his three seasons at Portman Road. He was voted Player of the Year in his first season with the Tractor Boys and selected for the PFA Championship Team of the Year in his final last season there.

Joining West Ham in 2014, Cresswell was an instant success and by November 2016 was capped by England against Spain at Wembley. A dead-ball specialist, his goal against Manchester City in 2018 illustrated the attacking quality he adds to being a solid full-back.

SQUAD NO:	**3**
POSITION:	Defender
DoB:	15 December 1989
BIRTHPLACE:	Liverpool

FABIAN
BALBUENA

Paraguay international centre-back Balbuena made the big switch to play in Europe with West Ham just as he turned 27. His big move came after two stunningly successful years in Brazil.

The Campeonato Paulista is the top level professional league in the Brazilian state of Sao Paulo. Balbuena had been selected for the Campeonato Paulista Team of the Year just before coming to West Ham. The previous year he had won a similar award in the Campeonato Brasileiro Team of the Year, when he also took the individual accolade.

In 2018, Fabian helped Corinthians retain the Campeonato Paulista which he had helped them to win the season before as well. These were the latest title wins for Balbuena in a career which has also seen him triumph with Libertad of Paraguay in 2014, three years after he won his home country's second tier with his first club Cerro Porteno. He has also played for Rubio Nu in his own country and Nacional of Uruguay.

SQUAD NO:	**4**
POSITION:	Defender
DoB:	23 August 1991
BIRTHPLACE:	Ciudad del Este, Paraguay

PABLO
ZABALETA

If you want pedigree, Pablo Zabaleta is absolutely top class. His 50 plus caps for Argentina include starting in the 2014 World Cup final, while in English football, Pablo has two Premier League winner's medals from his time with Manchester City, as well as FA Cup and League Cup winner's medals. He was also named in the PFA Team of the Year for the Premier League in 2012/13.

Now in his second season with the Irons, Zabaleta is approaching veteran status as he will be 34 early in 2019. The experience he has makes him a valuable member of the squad and indeed his total of 3,291 playing minutes was more than any of his teammates in his first season with West Ham.

Starting with San Lorenzo in Argentina, he moved to Europe with Espanyol after captaining Argentina to the World Youth Championship in 2005. In Spain, he won the Copa del Rey and reached the UEFA Cup final where his side lost on penalties to Seville.

SQUAD NO:	**5**
POSITION:	Defender
DoB:	16 January 1985
BIRTHPLACE:	Buenos Aires, Argentina

MARKO ARNAUTOVIC

SQUAD NO:	**7**
POSITION:	Forward
DoB:	19 April 1989
BIRTHPLACE:	Floridsdorf, Austria

When you pay a club record fee, you look for a player who can make an impact. In walking away with the Hammer of the Year award in his first season, Arnautovic amply illustrated he was worth the investment of his big money move from Stoke City.

Eleven goals and eight assists in his first campaign showed that in addition to the eye-catching skills and spectacular strikes, Marko is all about end product.

An international with Austria, he has over 70 caps and well over a one in four scoring record for his country. In his youth, Marko switched clubs frequently in and around Vienna representing Floridsdorfer AC, FK Austria Wien, First Vienna and Rapid Vienna, before a move to the Netherlands with FC Twente, playing for Jong FC Twente for whom he scored close to a goal a game.

After breaking into the Twente first team, he played briefly on loan to Inter Milan and had three years in Germany with Werder Bremen before joining Stoke in 2013.

FELIPE
ANDERSON

SQUAD NO:	**8**
POSITION:	Forward
DoB:	15 April 1993
BIRTHPLACE:	Santa Maria DF, Brazil

Signed in the summer of 2018 for a club record fee from Lazio, Brazil international Anderson is an attacking talent who can destroy teams from the wing and has the versatility to operate in various attacking roles. His pace, ball control and industriousness make him a valuable asset in the Irons' attacking armoury.

Felipe played for five clubs in Brazil as a young player, before settling on Pele's old club Santos where he made his senior debut on 6 October 2010, as a late sub in a win over Fluminense. Going on to play alongside Neymar, Anderson showed that Neymar was not the only star in town, eventually sealing a move to Lazio in June 2013 having won the Copa Libertadores and Recopa Sudamericana in South America.

In Italy, Felipe won the Italian Supercup with Lazio and returned to Brazil in 2016 to represent his country in the 2016 Olympics where he won a Gold Medal.

24

WEST HAM UNITED LONDON

SQUAD NO	**9**
POSITION:	Forward
DoB:	6 January 1989
BIRTHPLACE:	Gateshead

When fit, Andy Carroll is a fearsome centre-forward, capable of being totally dominant in the air and also able to score spectacularly with an athleticism not often gifted to someone of his height.

Carroll played in a Championship winning side with his first club Newcastle United in 2010 when he was included in the PFA Championship team of the year. The following January, Carroll moved to Liverpool for £35m, making him the costliest British player at the time. He won the League Cup and scored in the FA Cup final while with the Anfield club during the 2011/12 season. During the same campaign he scored his two full international goals, one against Ghana at Wembley, the other in the summer against Sweden at Euro 2012.

That summer, West Ham were able to acquire Andy initially on loan for a season. Following a successful season the Irons stepped in to complete the transfer. To the start of the 2018/19 season, Andy had scored 33 goals in 128 games for West Ham. As a youngster he also had a loan spell with Preston North End.

ANDY
CARROLL

MANUEL LANZINI

SQUAD NO: **10**
POSITION: Midfield
DoB: 15 February 1993
BIRTHPLACE: Buenos Aires, Argentina

When Lanzini sparkles, he lives up to his nick-name of 'La Joya' which in Spanish means 'The Jewel'. When Lanzini's quick-feet twinkle, he is an exciting player to watch. His ability to open up defences and score himself make Manuel a player of talent and terrific technique.

Players' Player of the Year at West Ham in 2017 shortly before he won his first full cap for Argentina, Lanzini has won league titles in Brazil and Argentina with Fluminense and River Plate in 2012 and 2014 respectively, the Brazilian honour coming while he was on loan from River.

Leaving South America in 2014 'The Jewel' went to the Middle East, being a marquee signing for Al Jazira Club in the UAE Arabian Gulf League, where instead of being a big-name veteran coming into the league, Manuel arrived as an up and coming 21-year old. After a year in the Middle East, Lanzini came to West Ham, initially on a season-long loan before completing his move in the summer of 2016.

ROBERT SNODGRASS

WEST HAM UNITED LONDON

SQUAD NO:	**11**
POSITION:	Midfield
DoB:	7 September 1987
BIRTHPLACE:	Glasgow

Set-piece specialist, capable of quality deliveries, Snodgrass started with Livingston and played for Stirling Albion on loan before crossing the border to join then League One Leeds United in 2008. A promotion winner in his second season in England, Robert made the PFA League One team of the Season.

Progress continued as he became captain under the management of Neil Warnock, broke into the Scotland squad and became the club's Player of the Year in 2012, prior to a transfer to Norwich where he was runner-up as Player of the Year in his first season at Carrow Road.

After two years at the club, Robert joined Hull City before he moved on to West Ham in January 2017 after three and a half seasons with the Tigers. Almost all of what looked like being his first full season with the Irons ended up being spent on loan to Villa, but a fresh start with West Ham saw him score twice in an 8-0 Carabao Cup win over Macclesfield. He now tops 500 career appearances, 100 goals and over 25 caps.

27

ADRIAN

SQUAD NO:	**13**
POSITION:	Goalkeeper
DoB:	3 January 1987
BIRTHPLACE:	Seville, Spain

Full name Adrian San Miguel del Castillo, the Spanish stopper has saved West Ham on numerous occasions and famously once won the game when he converted the decisive penalty in a shoot-out in an FA Cup tie against Everton in 2015. Playing as a striker up to the age of 10 with CD Altair obviously came in handy!

Adrian spent seven years from 2006-2013 with Real Betis in his home city of Seville. Working his way through Betis C and B teams, he had loans with Alcala and Utrera before making his La Liga debut in September 2012. Within two months he was keeping a clean sheet and walking away with the Man of the Match award against Real Madrid. It was one of twelve clean sheets Adrian kept in 32 La Liga games before coming to London in 2013 and winning the 2013/14 club Save of the Season award for a spectacular tip-over from Chelsea's Oscar.

Now a Spain international, Adrian started the 2018/19 campaign three games short of the 150 mark for the Irons.

PEDRO OBIANG

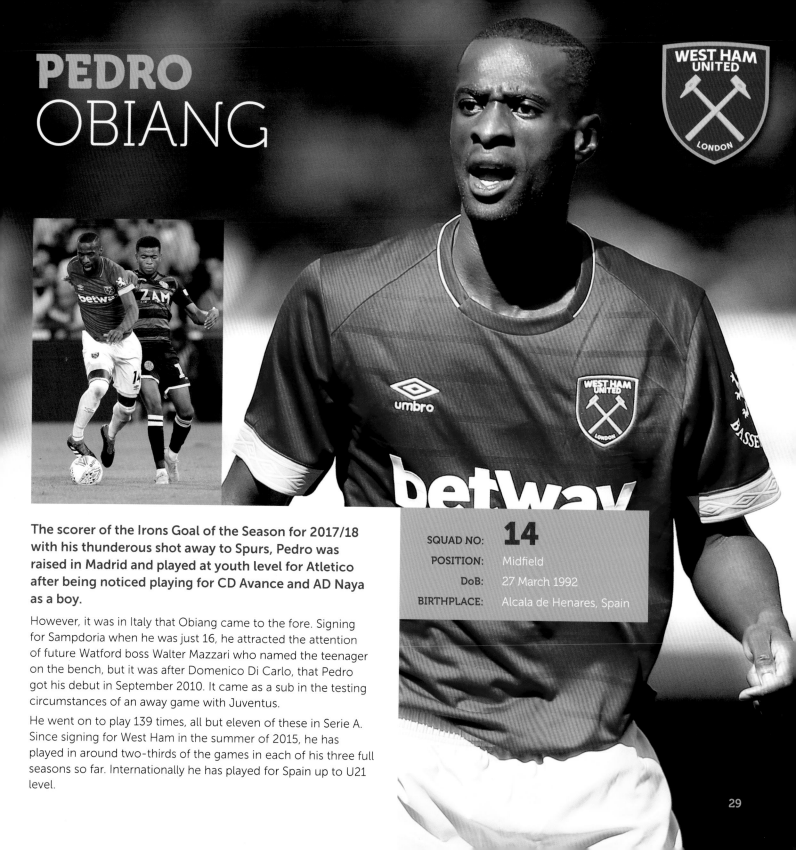

The scorer of the Irons Goal of the Season for 2017/18 with his thunderous shot away to Spurs, Pedro was raised in Madrid and played at youth level for Atletico after being noticed playing for CD Avance and AD Naya as a boy.

However, it was in Italy that Obiang came to the fore. Signing for Sampdoria when he was just 16, he attracted the attention of future Watford boss Walter Mazzari who named the teenager on the bench, but it was after Domenico Di Carlo, that Pedro got his debut in September 2010. It came as a sub in the testing circumstances of an away game with Juventus.

He went on to play 139 times, all but eleven of these in Serie A. Since signing for West Ham in the summer of 2015, he has played in around two-thirds of the games in each of his three full seasons so far. Internationally he has played for Spain up to U21 level.

SQUAD NO:	**14**
POSITION:	Midfield
DoB:	27 March 1992
BIRTHPLACE:	Alcala de Henares, Spain

CARLOS
SANCHEZ

The experienced central-midfielder who joined West Ham in the summer of 2018 has over 80 caps for Colombia, playing at the last two World Cups as well as in three Copa America tournaments.

After developing at Danubio, a team in the Uruguayan capital of Montevideo, Sanchez started his senior career in the same city with River Plate, before coming to European football with Valenciennes in France. In 2013 Carlos crossed the border to Spain to sign for Elche moving on a year later, this time to Aston Villa.

Sanchez came on as a sub against Arsenal in the FA Cup final in 2015, but moved on again after two years in the midlands. This time on loan to Fiorentina in Italy before having another taste of Spanish soccer on loan with RCD Espanyol before coming to West Ham.

Debuting for the Irons against Bournemouth in August, Carlos gradually settled into the side and first appeared in a winning side in the 8-0 Carabao Cup hammering of Macclesfield.

SQUAD NO:	**15**
POSITION:	Midfield
DoB:	6 February 1986
BIRTHPLACE:	Quibdo, Colombia

30

MARK
NOBLE

WEST HAM UNITED LONDON

SQUAD NO:	**16**
POSITION:	Midfield
DoB:	8 May 1987
BIRTHPLACE:	Canning Town

Since debuting in August 2004 as a 17-year-old, Mark Noble has become an essential part of the fabric of West Ham United. Twice Hammer of the Year in 2012 and 2014, Noble has also twice been a promotion-winner with his club, being named in the PFA Championship Team of the Year in 2012.

A one-club man, albeit he had loan spells with Hull City and Ipswich Town during his development years, Mark has played for England 47 times at various levels, captaining his country at U21 level - but to the surprise of many, is yet to win a full cap.

Skipper of the Irons in the Boleyn Ground's final fixture, Mark had a Testimonial in March 2016 against a West Ham All-Stars side. Two months later, Noble's dedication and loyalty was further recognized when he was granted the Freedom of the Borough of Newham.

JAVIER HERNANDEZ

SQUAD NO:	**17**
POSITION:	Forward
DoB:	1 June 1988
BIRTHPLACE:	Guadalajara, Jalisco, Mexico

Javier Hernandez Balcazar is better known in football as 'Chicarito' which means Little Pea. Mexico's all-time record scorer has played at six major tournaments for the South American country, including the World Cup finals in 2014 and 2010.

Scoring against France in 2010, he emulated his grandfather Tomas Balcazar, who scored against France for Mexico in the 1954 finals. Chicarito added another goal in the tournament against Argentina and netted against Croatia in the 2014 finals.

Goals run in the family; Little Pea's father, Javier Hernandez Gutierrez was a member of Mexico's 1986 World Cup squad. The nickname comes from his dad who was known as Chicharo - meaning pea - because of his sparkling green eyes.

The modern day West ham striker has a host of individual honours won for club and country as part of a personal trophy collection which includes winning the FIFA Club World Cup with Real Madrid, two Premier League titles with Manchester United and the Mexican Primera Division. He has also played in Germany with Bayer Leverkusen.

JACK
WILSHERE

One of the most accomplished English midfielders of his generation, Jack has over 30 caps for his country and has experienced being part of the squad at both the European Championships and World Cup.

An Irons fan as a boy, Wilshere came to West Ham in the summer of 2018 after 17 years associated with Arsenal, where he twice won the FA Cup having earlier also twice won the FA Youth Cup. He had also become the youngest player to ever represent the Gunners in league football, making his league debut at the age of just 16 years and 256 days.

Jack has had two loans during his career, playing for Bolton Wanderers in 2010 and AFC Bournemouth in 2016/17. A creative player always looking for the telling penetrating pass, Wilshere also has a goal in him, but as a complete modern midfielder, he is also a player who likes to be a ball winner and can play with a bit of an edge.

SQUAD NO:	**19**
POSITION:	Midfield
DoB:	1 January 1992
BIRTHPLACE:	Stevenage

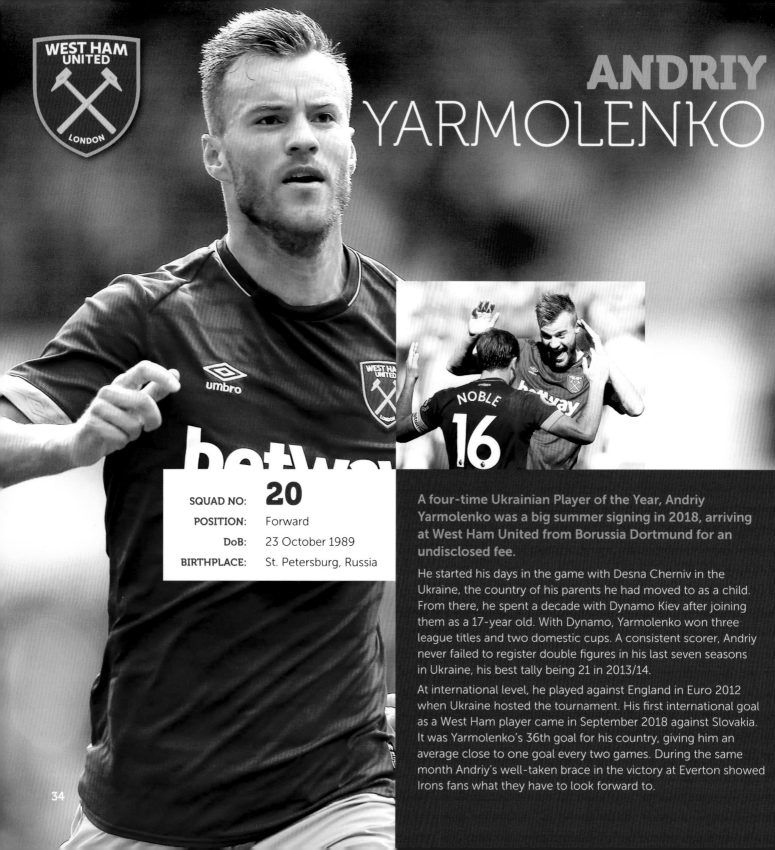

ANDRIY YARMOLENKO

SQUAD NO:	**20**
POSITION:	Forward
DoB:	23 October 1989
BIRTHPLACE:	St. Petersburg, Russia

A four-time Ukrainian Player of the Year, Andriy Yarmolenko was a big summer signing in 2018, arriving at West Ham United from Borussia Dortmund for an undisclosed fee.

He started his days in the game with Desna Cherniv in the Ukraine, the country of his parents he had moved to as a child. From there, he spent a decade with Dynamo Kiev after joining them as a 17-year old. With Dynamo, Yarmolenko won three league titles and two domestic cups. A consistent scorer, Andriy never failed to register double figures in his last seven seasons in Ukraine, his best tally being 21 in 2013/14.

At international level, he played against England in Euro 2012 when Ukraine hosted the tournament. His first international goal as a West Ham player came in September 2018 against Slovakia. It was Yarmolenko's 36th goal for his country, giving him an average close to one goal every two games. During the same month Andriy's well-taken brace in the victory at Everton showed Irons fans what they have to look forward to.

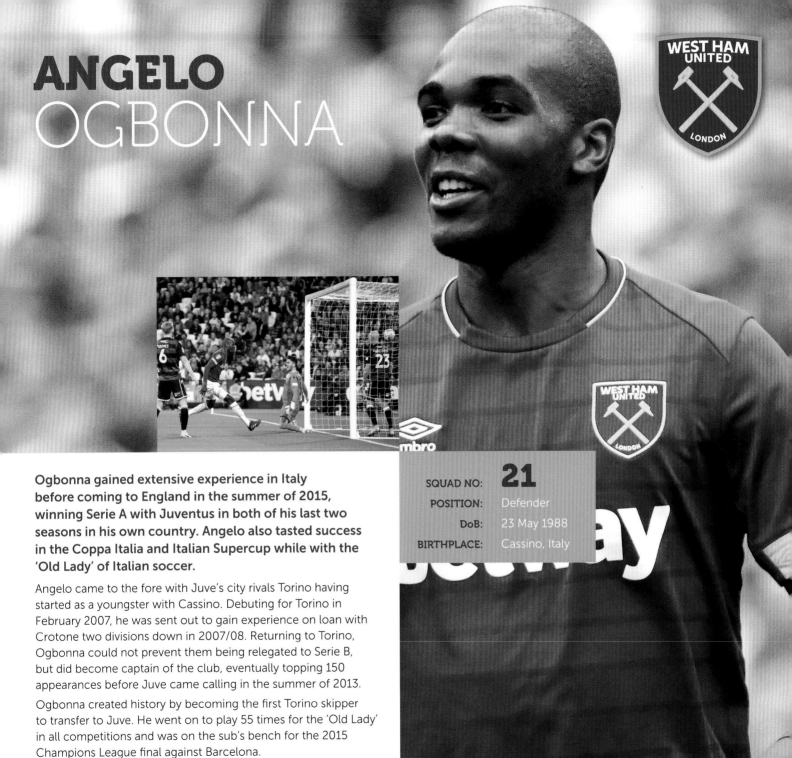

ANGELO OGBONNA

Ogbonna gained extensive experience in Italy before coming to England in the summer of 2015, winning Serie A with Juventus in both of his last two seasons in his own country. Angelo also tasted success in the Coppa Italia and Italian Supercup while with the 'Old Lady' of Italian soccer.

Angelo came to the fore with Juve's city rivals Torino having started as a youngster with Cassino. Debuting for Torino in February 2007, he was sent out to gain experience on loan with Crotone two divisions down in 2007/08. Returning to Torino, Ogbonna could not prevent them being relegated to Serie B, but did become captain of the club, eventually topping 150 appearances before Juve came calling in the summer of 2013.

Ogbonna created history by becoming the first Torino skipper to transfer to Juve. He went on to play 55 times for the 'Old Lady' in all competitions and was on the sub's bench for the 2015 Champions League final against Barcelona.

An international with Italy, Angelo was in the squad for the last two European Championships.

SQUAD NO:	**21**
POSITION:	Defender
DoB:	23 May 1988
BIRTHPLACE:	Cassino, Italy

35

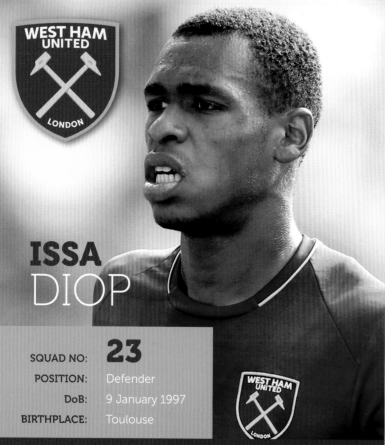

ISSA DIOP

SQUAD NO:	**23**
POSITION:	Defender
DoB:	9 January 1997
BIRTHPLACE:	Toulouse

After seeing his Manchester United side outplayed and defeated at the London Stadium at the end of September, Jose Mourinho proclaimed, "Congratulations to the scout who found the 21-year old kid, Diop, a monster who dominated everything in the duels."

In fact, Mourinho's own club were one of several to monitor the 'monster' at his first club Toulouse. Barcelona, Arsenal, Spurs, Fulham, Everton, Dortmund and Seville were amongst the other clubs reported to be interested in the 6' 4" centre-back, but it was West Ham who matched interest with ambition, investing a reported £22m, having reportedly been alerted by Mark McKay, the same man who brought Dimitri Payet to the Irons' attention.

The grandson of the first Senegalese player in Ligue 1 (Lybasse Diop of Bordeaux), Issa is eligible for Senegal, his mother's birthplace of Morocco and France who he has represented up to U21 level.

Manuel Pellegrini's first signing for the club, Fredericks enjoyed an outstanding season with Fulham in 2017/18. He was named in the Championship Team of the Year having helped the Craven Cottage club to promotion.

Capped by England at U19 level, Ryan has the pace to cause problems, bursting forward from right-back or right-wing-back. He came through the academy system at Spurs, getting 35 league games under his belt via loans with Brentford, Millwall and Middlesbrough, making an increased number of games with each loan. Although he did not add to his league experience with Tottenham, he did play cup football for them.

A false start at Bristol City saw Fredericks sign for the Robins in August 2015, but leave for Fulham after just 26 days and five games. Totalling 32, 34 and 48 appearances in his three seasons with Fulham, Fredericks is coming into what should be the peak years of his career which he will spend with the Irons.

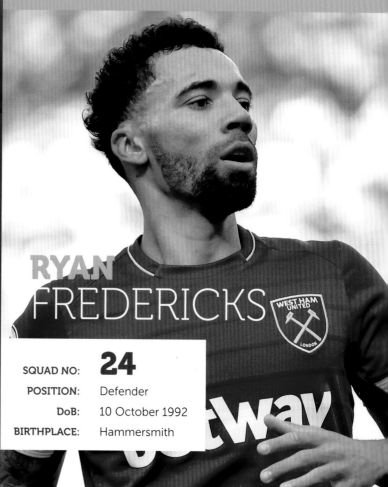

RYAN FREDERICKS

SQUAD NO:	**24**
POSITION:	Defender
DoB:	10 October 1992
BIRTHPLACE:	Hammersmith

Arthur's career started in his home town as a boy with Lille OM and a spell at RC Lens prior to breaking into senior football with a debut on the opening day of the 2013/14 season with Valenciennes.

An impressive first season led to a transfer to Greece with Olympiacos for whom he played Champions League football, even scoring against the notoriously tight defence of Atletico Madrid. A league title winner in each of his two seasons with Olympiacos, he also won the domestic cup and was a cup runner-up during his Mediterranean experience. Seventy-four games spread over two years preceded a move to West Ham in 2016 for a fee reported to be over £6m.

Settling into the physical rigours of English football, Masuaku more than doubled the 15 appearances he managed in his first season in his second campaign. A former France U19 international, as a senior player, Masuaku has been selected for DR Congo.

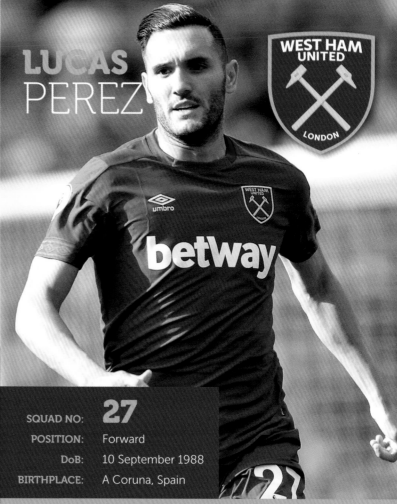

LUCAS PEREZ

SQUAD NO:	**27**
POSITION:	Forward
DoB:	10 September 1988
BIRTHPLACE:	A Coruna, Spain

Signed from Arsenal ahead of the 2018/19 season, Perez is a forward who provides options because of his ability to operate in a range of attacking positions.

Comfortable as a 'number 10', leading the line, playing off the centre-forward or even out wide, Perez is an experienced player who is an astute addition to the Irons squad.

As a youngster, Lucas started with Atletico Madrid, playing for their C team before moving on to Rayo Vallecano, winning promotion with their B team in 2010 and earning a first-team debut. In 2011, he was transferred to FC Karpaty Lviv in Ukraine. Averaging exactly a goal every four appearances, he moved on to Dynamo Kiev in 2012/13 for a loan spell where he teamed up with Andriy Yarmolenko.

Before coming to England Perez also played in Greece with PAOK and had a further spell in Spain with Deportivo La Coruna.

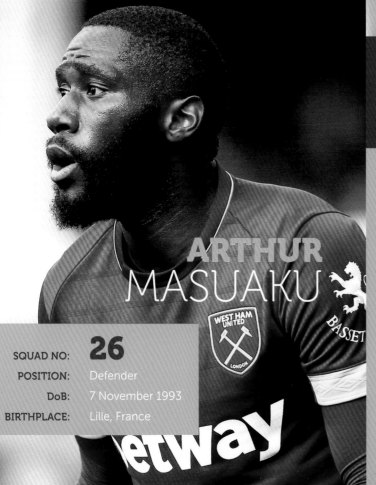

ARTHUR MASUAKU

SQUAD NO:	**26**
POSITION:	Defender
DoB:	7 November 1993
BIRTHPLACE:	Lille, France

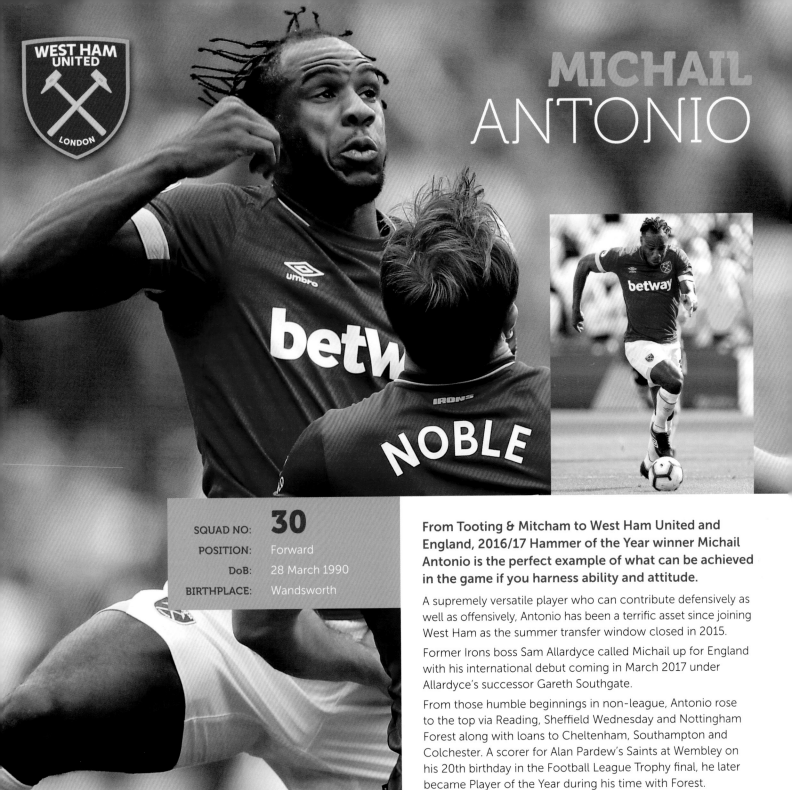

MICHAIL ANTONIO

SQUAD NO:	**30**
POSITION:	Forward
DoB:	28 March 1990
BIRTHPLACE:	Wandsworth

From Tooting & Mitcham to West Ham United and England, 2016/17 Hammer of the Year winner Michail Antonio is the perfect example of what can be achieved in the game if you harness ability and attitude.

A supremely versatile player who can contribute defensively as well as offensively, Antonio has been a terrific asset since joining West Ham as the summer transfer window closed in 2015.

Former Irons boss Sam Allardyce called Michail up for England with his international debut coming in March 2017 under Allardyce's successor Gareth Southgate.

From those humble beginnings in non-league, Antonio rose to the top via Reading, Sheffield Wednesday and Nottingham Forest along with loans to Cheltenham, Southampton and Colchester. A scorer for Alan Pardew's Saints at Wembley on his 20th birthday in the Football League Trophy final, he later became Player of the Year during his time with Forest.

Still a teenager until under two weeks before Christmas 2018, it seems as if Oxford has been around for years. He has. Reece was only 15 when he first appeared on the bench in a League Cup tie against Sheffield United in the opening month of the 2014/15 season.

Reece waited almost a year from that first time on the bench to actually getting on the pitch, but when he did so against FC Lusitans on 2 July 2015, he still became the youngest player ever to play for West Ham, at the age of 16 and 198 days. He did so well that he started the opening Premier League game of that season at Arsenal.

Capped by England at all levels from U16 to U20, Oxford has added to his experience in recent years with loans to Reading and two spells in Germany with Borussia Monchengladbach.

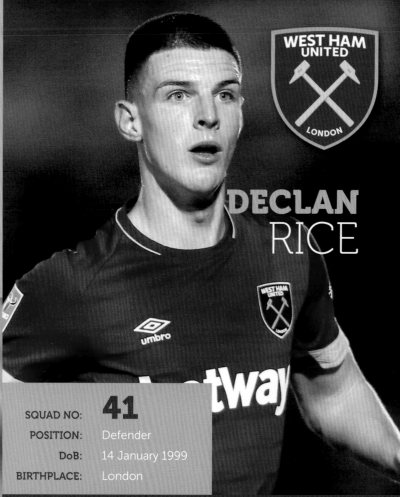

DECLAN RICE

SQUAD NO:	**41**
POSITION:	Defender
DoB:	14 January 1999
BIRTHPLACE:	London

Man of the Match at Wembley at the start of 2018 in the game when Pedro Obiang scored the Irons' Goal of the Season, Declan Rice was West Ham's Young Player of the Year in both 2017 and 2018, as well as being runner up to Marko Arnautovic as Hammer of the Year in 2018.

Released by Chelsea at the age of 14 having been with the Blues since he was seven, Rice made his Irons debut against Burnley at the end of the 2016/17 season, getting the briefest of tastes of the big time after coming off the bench in injury time.

Qualifying via County Cork-born grandparents, Declan made his full international debut for the Republic of Ireland in March 2018 after representing Ireland at U16, U17, U19 and U21 levels. However, having played three full internationals for Ireland in friendlies, he remains eligible for England.

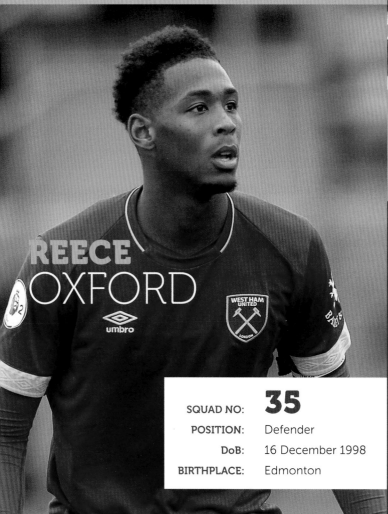

REECE OXFORD

SQUAD NO:	**35**
POSITION:	Defender
DoB:	16 December 1998
BIRTHPLACE:	Edmonton

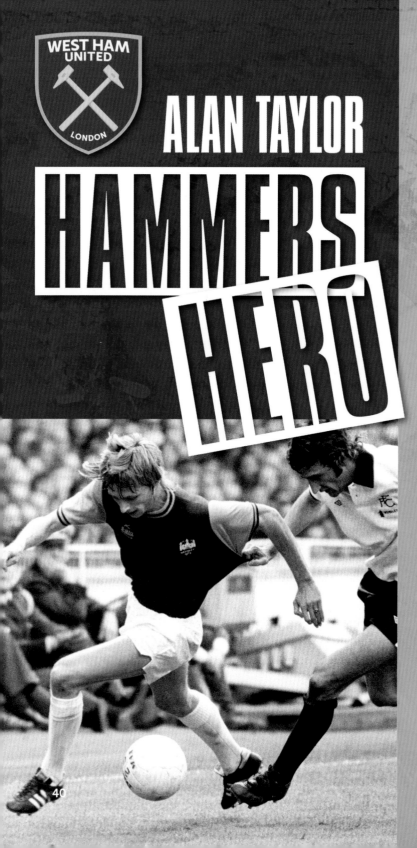

ALAN TAYLOR

HAMMERS HERO

Striker Alan Taylor has legendary status at West Ham United after scoring both goals in the Hammers' 1975 FA Cup Final victory over Fulham.

Signed by John Lyall in November 1974 from Rochdale - for a fee of £40,000 - Taylor's goals proved to be the driving force in the latter stages of the club's 1974/75 FA Cup campaign.

However, it could all have been so different had injury not have prevented him from playing for Dale in the first round of the competition. Little did he know at the time, but had he been fit to face Marine in the first round prior to his move to East London, then he would have been cup-tied and ineligible to feature for the Hammers.

With an impressive record of a goal in every three games for Rochdale, his £40,000 switch to Upton Park created a then club record sale for the Spotland club.

Taylor made his Hammers' debut in a 2-1 First Division victory over Leeds United in December 1974. In only his second start in a West Ham shirt, Taylor won the hearts of the Hammers fans when he scored both goals in the FA Cup quarter-final victory over Arsenal at Highbury. He followed up his Highbury brace with goals in the next two league fixtures as West Ham beat Burnley at Upton Park and then drew 1-1 away to Birmingham City. The striker certainly displayed little difficulty in swiftly stepping up from the Fourth Division to the top flight.

Taylor was once again the cup hero as the Hammers booked their place in the final. After the initial semi-final against Ipswich Town ended goalless, Taylor netted twice in the Stamford Bridge replay to seal a 2-0 win and secure an FA Cup final date with Fulham.

The 1975 FA Cup Final is that match which Taylor is always so fondly remembered for. His two second-half goals ensured West Ham won the match 2-0 and lifted the famous old trophy for the second time in the club's history.

Taylor was the club's leading scorer in 1975/76 with 17 goals and was on target in the memorable European Cup Winners' Cup campaign. He netted against Ararat Erevan in the second round and Den Haag in round three, before appearing in the final as a substitute when he replaced Frank Lampard.

In total, Taylor scored 36 goals for West Ham in 124 games for the club. His final game for the Hammers came on 5 May 1979 away to Blackburn Rovers. He then joined Norwich City later that summer.

Taylor twice tried his luck in Canada at Vancouver Whitecaps, with a spell at Cambridge United sandwiched inbetween. He also played league football at Hull City, Burnley and Bury before returning to Carrow Road for a second spell with Norwich City in 1988/89 and then retiring from the game.

He remains an extremely popular guest whenever he returns to West Ham from his Norfolk home for matches or reunion events.

FULL NAME:	Alan David Taylor
DATE OF BIRTH:	14 November 1953
PLACE OF BIRTH:	Hinckley
POSITION:	Striker

HAMMERS APPEARANCES	HAMMERS GOALS
124	**36**
LEAGUE: 98	LEAGUE: 25
FA CUP: 8	FA CUP: 6
LEAGUE CUP: 8	LEAGUE CUP: 2
OTHER: 10	OTHER: 3

DEBUT: West Ham United 2 Leeds Utd 1
7 December 1974 · Division One

HAMMERS LEADING GOALSCORER: 1975/1976
17 Goals

Very much a season of two halves, the first part of the 2017/18 campaign was a struggle. It was a struggle that resulted in the demise of Slaven Bilic who parted company with the Hammers on 6 November to be replaced by David Moyes a day later.

2017/18 REVIEW

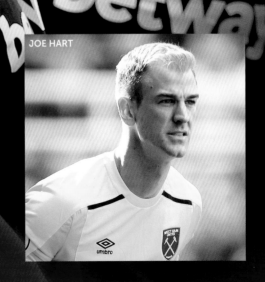

JOE HART

Moyes lifted the Irons from 17th place when he took over to a final berth of 13th with the help of seven points from the final three games. Ultimately his dour approach was not right for a club proud of its creativity and style, and his tenure ended as the season closed.

Bilic had been well backed in the transfer market. Austria international Marko Arnautovic arrived from Stoke City for £20m, with a further £16m spent on Javier Hernandez of Bayer Leverkusen. While they were the headline buys, Argentina international Pablo Zabaleta was also acquired from Manchester City, midfielder Anouar El Mhassani came in from Ajax and another midfielder Sead Haksabanovic arrived from Swedish outfit Halmstads.

Sixteen-year-old El Mhassani was one for the future, as was Haksabanovic. Of more immediate impact was a player who arrived on loan, goalkeeper Joe Hart from Manchester City. Hart had a hard time in E20 though and was quickly dropped by Moyes.

The first three games ended in defeat, ten goals being conceded on the road before a home game was possible. Two goals in five minutes mid-way through the second half from Pedro Obiang and Andre Ayew lifted spirits as Huddersfield were beaten to kick-start the season as only one Premier League game in five was lost.

ANGELO OGBONNA NETS THE THIRD AGAINST SPURS AT WEMBLEY IN THE LEAGUE CUP

Despite a draw at Crystal Palace and a sensational fightback in front of a less than half-full Wembley, as a 2-0 League Cup half-time deficit in the Carabao Cup against Tottenham was turned into a 3-2 win, heavy home defeats in the next two home games, a 3-0 reverse to Brighton and a 4-1 loss to Liverpool, signalled the end for Bilic.

A DELIGHTED PEDRO OBIANG CELEBRATES SCORING AT HOME TO HUDDERSFIELD TOWN

MARK NOBLE ON TARGET AT HUDDERSFIELD TOWN

CELEBRATIONS AFTER MANUEL LANZINI GRABS THE THIRD AT HUDDERSFIELD

Appointed at the beginning of an international break, Moyes had the opportunity to work with his new side before the action restarted, but began with a 2-0 defeat at Watford, a disappointing home draw with Leicester City and a 4-0 thumping at his old club Everton.

Having been less than impressive in his last three appointments at Sunderland, Real Sociedad and Manchester United, Moyes' return to Goodison, where he spent eleven years, provided a personal low point for the manager. The Irons, who had slumped into the relegation positions after Moyes' first game, were showing no sign of escaping it any time soon.

The next game at Manchester City looked daunting, but with on loan Joe Hart unable to play against his parent club, Moyes had no choice but to restore Adrian between the sticks. The goalkeeper did so well, champions-elect City only edged the game with a late winner. Keeping his place, Adrian kept three successive clean sheets as seven points were earned, lifting the club to 15th in the table.

Rather than stick with Adrian, Moyes brought back Hart into a much-changed team as the Hammers slipped out of the Carabao Cup, missing the chance to reach the semi-finals as the home side made eleven changes from their previous league match. Adrian was restored for the next league game, a home defeat to a Newcastle side who had taken only one point from their previous nine games. Thankfully, things improved with a run of four draws and two wins, including the completion of the double over Huddersfield Town with a 4-1 away triumph.

By the end of January, a season high of tenth was reached, but the pendulum swung back with three defeats in four, eight goals conceded in the last two of those leading to the restoration of Hart once again. It made little difference. A 3-0 home defeat to Burnley before the start of an international break increased anxiety as the team were looking over their shoulders in 16th place.

AN ELATED MARKO ARNAUTOVIC WITH TEAMMATES
ARTHUR MASUAKU AND AARON CRESSWELL AFTER
HIS GOAL V CHELSEA AT LONDON STADIUM

2017/18 REVIEW

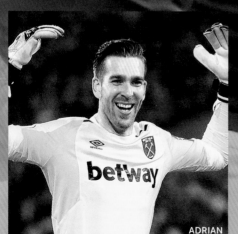

ADRIAN

WEST HAM UNITED
LONDON

2017/18 REVIEW

JOAO MARIO SCORING AT LEICESTER CITY
...AND SOUTHAMPTON

In January, Moyes had brought in Jordan Hugill from Preston. He failed to score in the three games he was given, but Portuguese midfielder Joao Mario, who had arrived on loan from Inter, came up with a vital goal that opened the scoring against struggling Southampton. Arnautovic finished the job off with a brace.

A hard-fought point at Chelsea was followed by another crucial draw at home to Stoke, where Andy Carroll's last minute equaliser was one of the Geordie's rare, but important contributions.

ANDY CARROLL'S LEVELLER AGAINST STOKE CITY

Coming into the home straight, Moyes again changed keepers through necessity. Although having leaked four in a defeat at Arsenal, Hart may well have been left out even if the next match was not against his parent club. When Adrian was also beaten four times at home to Manchester City, it was the seventh time four goals had been conceded in a game.

It was at this point that Joao Mario again opened the scoring to set up a 2-0 victory at Leicester. The final two games of the season were both at home as the Hammers ended the campaign on a high note. A point was taken from the visit of Manchester United before the Toffees were beaten 3-1 in what proved to be Moyes' last match in charge and also former Irons boss Sam Allardyce's final game in the Everton hot-seat.

In the end, a mid-table finish of 13th along with a run to the Carabao Cup quarter-final was not such a bad season, but one the Irons will be determined to improve on.

MANUEL LANZINI LEAPS FOR JOY ON PABLO ZABALETA V EVERTON

THE MOMENT

Argentinean star Carlos Tevez was the Hammers' hero of the hour as he helped inspire Premier League survival

FIXTURE	Premier League
DATE:	Sunday 13 May 2007
SCORE:	Man Utd 0-1 West Ham United
VENUE:	Old Trafford
ATTENDANCE:	75,927

West Ham United went into the final game of the 2006/07 campaign with their Premier League status hanging by a thread.

The final round of fixtures saw the Hammers face the toughest of challenges away to Champions Manchester United. Alan Curbishley's men headed off to Old Trafford knowing they needed a point to ensure Premier League football at Upon Park in 2007/08.

Against a United side who were celebrating their 16th English league title, the Hammers remained focused on winning the all-important point that would guarantee top-light status.

The Hammers started confidently enough, but it was the champions who had the first clear opportunity when Wayne Rooney squandered a great chance to open the scoring after Darren Fletcher's through-ball.

Wes Brown was twice called into action at the other end to clear his lines as Curbishley's men showed plenty of willingness to attack. However, the home side looked the more likely to break through and Rooney, Alan Smith and Ole Gunnar Solskjaer all had half-chances as West Ham held firm.

Yossi Benayoun rescued West Ham twice in a matter of seconds when he first headed Smith's flicked effort off the line, then stood firm as Kieran Richardson let fly with the rebound. Robert Green then made a superb fingertip save to deny John O'Shea.

Carlos Tevez then fired West Ham into the lead in injury time, the home defence failed to deal with Green's long punt down field and, after exchanging passes with Bobby Zamora, Tevez squeezed his shot home.

As the second half progressed, the Red Devils continued to struggle to make any headway and Sir Alex Ferguson made a triple substitution before the hour mark with Patrice Evra, Michael Carrick and Alan Smith replaced by Ryan Giggs, Paul Scholes and Cristiano Ronaldo.

The Hammers were forced back by wave after wave of attacks, but the visitors stood firm to pull-off an amazing relegation escape and spoil the Old Trafford title party.

The final whistle signalled the culmination of a six-week-long miracle relegation escape for the Hammers, and Tevez was the toast of Upton Park as the club maintained its top-flight status.

WEST HAM
UNITED

LONDON

45'

VAN DER SAR ①　㉜ TEVEZ

㉜ TEVEZ

㉕ ZAMORA

㉕ ZAMORA

TEVEZ ㉜

TEVEZ ㉜

<<REWIND

QUIZ OF THE YEAR

2017/18 was another eventful campaign for the Irons. What can you recall? Here are 20 teasers to tackle...

1

Name the German club that West Ham United faced in the in the 2017/18 Betway Cup during the club's pre-season preparations?

From which club did the Hammers sign Mexican striker Javier Hernandez in July 2017?

2

3

Which fixture proved to be Slaven Bilic's final game in charge of the club?

4

Goalkeeping duties fell to Adrian and on-loan stopper Joe Hart in 2017/18.

Of the 45 competitive games the Hammers played in all competitions, which of the two 'keepers made the most appearances?

5

Against which club did the Hammers record their first Premier League victory of the 2017/18 season?

6

The club recruited experienced Argentinean full-back Pablo Zabaleta from Manchester City ahead of the 2017/18 campaign.

How many times was Zabaleta a Premier League champion while at the Etihad?

7

At which venue did West Ham United win their first Premier League away fixture in 2017/18?

8

New boss David Moyes recorded his first win as West Ham United manager against which London rival?

9

Which former Hammer returned to the club as part of Moyes' backroom staff?

10

The Hammers produced a stunning comeback to knock Tottenham Hotspur out of the League Cup at Wembley Stadium.

Trailing 2-0 at the break, can you recall who scored the second-half goals to secure a 3-2 success?

11

Who knocked the Hammers out of the League Cup at the quarter-final stage?

13

Which player scored the first West Ham United goal of 2018?

12

Can you name the club the Hammers were drawn away to in the FA Cup third round?

14

Which West Ham United player was sent off in the Premier League match away to Burnley in October 2017?

16

Scotland international midfielder Robert Snodgrass spent the season on loan with which Championship club?

15

How many goals did Javier Hernandez net during his debut season at the club?

Was it eight, nine or ten?

17

From which club did the Hammers loan Joao Mario in the 2018 January transfer window?

19

Leading marksman Marko Arnautovic was voted Hammer of the Year in 2017/18. How many goals did he score during the season?

18

The season ended with a 3-1 win over which of Moyes' former clubs?

20

Who was runner-up in the 2017/18 Hammer of the Year voting?

ANSWERS ON PAGE 82

51

The Hammers' faithful following have witnessed countless great goals over the years and while this selection may not be the definitive compilation of the club's best ten goals,

hopefully they will stir a few memories...

1. FELIPE ANDERSON

WEST HAM UNITED 3-1 MANCHESTER UNITED
PREMIER LEAGUE · 29 SEPTEMBER 2018

Record signing Felipe Anderson picked the perfect moment to score his first competitive goal for West Ham United. After a tricky start to 2018/19, Anderson opened the scoring after just five minutes at London Stadium in the 3-1 win over Manchester United as the Hammers recorded their first home Premier League victory of the season.

The Brazilian winger's first goal in Claret and Blue was an audacious flicked volley from Pablo Zabaleta's cross which set the Hammers on their way to a tremendous victory, as they ended September 2018 in the best possible way.

The club-record signing was understandably delighted to play his part in a result which made it seven points out of a possible nine from three tough fixtures - away to Everton and at home to Chelsea and Manchester United.

"That was a match that we all wanted to win," he told West Ham TV. **"I'm always happy when I score, but when it comes to such a goal, the joy is greater.**

"I didn't have time to think, because I was making the move to enter the box when I saw Pablo's cross and I had to react immediately. The last touch is always instinctive, although sometimes results in a more difficult move. Luckily, in this case, I could finish it."

This match certainly saw the 25-year-old produce his best performance in a West Ham shirt and when he was replaced with just a few minutes to go, with Grady Diangana being handed a Premier League debut off the bench, Anderson received a rapturous reception as he left the pitch - with all inside London Stadium knowing the importance of that crucial opening goal.

10 GREAT GOALS

2. ANDY CARROLL

WEST HAM UNITED 3
CRYSTAL PALACE 0
PREMIER LEAGUE · 14 JANUARY 2017

When it came to awarding the Hammers' Goal of the Season accolade for 2016/17, there really was only ever one show in town, Andy Carroll's breathtaking scissor-kick in the Hammers' 3-0 defeat of London rivals Crystal Palace at London Stadium in January 2017.

Leading 1-0 thanks to Sofiane Feghouli's 68th minute opener, the hosts doubled their lead eleven minutes from time, but the goal itself was simply one of those 'I was there' moments as Carroll dispatched his stunning finish.

The goal was created down the left-hand channel as Manuel Lanzini combined with Michail Antonio who floated a cross into the Palace box where Carroll peeled away from his marker before unleashing a stunning mid-air volley that left visiting 'keeper Wayne Hennessey helpless.

The impressive facts behind the goal are that Carroll was 13.4 yards from goal when he struck the ball at a speed of 62.1 mph. Incredibly the ball was 5ft 10in off the ground when it left his boot and it took just 0.47 seconds to reach back of net.

With the stadium still buzzing from Carroll's wonder-strike, Lanzini wrapped up the win with the Hammers' third goal after 86 minutes.

3. DIMITRI PAYET

WEST HAM UNITED 1-1 MIDDLESBROUGH
PREMIER LEAGUE · 1 OCTOBER 2016

French magician Dimitri Payet lit up London Stadium with a skilful solo effort to salvage a draw from the Hammers' 2016/17 Premier League clash with Middlesbrough.

The point gained was certainly a welcome one for Slaven Bilic's side who had lost their previous four league outings. However, for fans fortunate enough to be inside London Stadium to have witnessed Payet's wonder-goal, concerns over current form would fall by the wayside as this was just a moment of pure individual brilliance that was a privilege to watch.

With his team trailing to a 51st minute Christian Stuani goal, Payet took possession on the left, having instantly controlled a long raking pass out of defence from Winston Reid. The Frenchman then turned past Antonio Barragan and then amazingly weaved his way across goal, past four defenders, before firing a low driven shot past Boro 'keeper Victor Valdes.

The goal was the work of a genius and an instant contender for Match of the Day's Goal of the Season award.

From his exquisite first touch and turn, to the confident surge into the area and the ability to evade so many opponents - this was a goal Hammers fans will never tire of watching time and time again.

4. CHEIKHOU KOUYATE

WEST HAM UNITED 3-0 NK DOMZALE

EUROPA LEAGUE · 4 AUGUST 2016

Cheikhou Kouyate wrote his name into the West Ham United history books when he netted the club's first goal at London Stadium in August 2016.

In front of a 54,000 crowd, the Hammers stepped out for the first time at their new home when they faced Slovenian side NK Domzale in a second leg, third round Europa League qualifying fixture.

Despite a first-half penalty from Mark Noble, a Matic Crnic double gave NK Domzale a 2-1 first-leg advantage. Things were set up perfectly for the club's eagerly-awaited opening game at London Stadium.

Kouyate wasted little time in ensuring this exciting new era of Hammers history got off to a perfect start as he opened the scoring with a neat back-healed goal after just eight minutes of action.

Enner Valencia broke away down the left and pulled the ball back to Sam Byram who in turn picked out Kouyate and the Senegal international produced a piece of quick thinking to instinctively flick the ball home.

Clearly enjoyed his new surroundings, Kouyate added his and West Ham's second goal after 25 minutes. Sofiane Feghouli struck in the final ten minutes to record 3-0 victory on a memorable evening as Slaven Bilic's men progressed 4-2 on aggregate.

5. WINSTON REID

WEST HAM UNITED 3-1 MANCHESTER UNITED
PREMIER LEAGUE · 10 MAY 2016

West Ham United produced a barnstorming performance to come from behind and defeat Manchester United in the club's final game at their Upton Park home.

On an emotional night in East London, the curtain came down on 112 years of football at the Boleyn Ground as Hammers defender Winston Reid took the mantle of scoring the final goal at the famous old ground.

The send off celebrations could not have really got off to a better start when Diafra Sakho slotted the Hammers in front after just ten minutes. After the break, Manchester United's Anthony Martial then looked to have spoilt the farewell party with two goals in 19 second-half minutes to turn the games in the visitors' favour. However, the home side then produced an incredible final 15 minutes of football for the fans to savour.

Firstly, Michail Antonio netted a 76th minute equaliser and then came the moment of the night as Reid headed home the winner with ten minutes left on the clock.

The final goal that triggered wild scenes of celebration came after Dimitri Payet sent a free-kick from the left into the box which Reid met with a rocket-like header that flew past David De Gea into the visitors' net.

6. RICARDO VAZ TE

WEST HAM UNITED 2-1 BLACKPOOL
CHAMPIONSHIP PLAY-OFF FINAL · 19 MAY 2012

Ricardo Vaz Te struck a late winner as West Ham United defeated Blackpool in an absorbing Championship Play-Off Final at Wembley to seal their return to the Premier League at the end of the 2011/12 campaign.

The result ensured manager Sam Allardyce made good on his promise to take the Hammers back into the top-flight after his team narrowly missed out on automatic promotion at the end of the regular season. Allardyce's side had led at the break through a Carlton Cole strike, but after Thomas Ince - son of former Hammers midfielder Paul - levelled shortly after the restart, the match became increasingly stretched and ragged.

Both teams wasted good opportunities to score, but it was the Hammers who did grab what proved to be the decisive third goal. The match seemed to be heading for extra-time, but when Blackpool 'keeper Matt Gilks parried at the feet of Cole, the unmarked Vaz Te was on hand to drill the ball into the Blackpool net from twelve yards.

The goal saw Vaz Te gain cult status among the West Ham fans as their team justified its pre-match billing as favourites and left supporters looking forward to a return to the Premier League.

DEAN ASHTON

MANCHESTER CITY 1
WEST HAM UNITED 2

FA CUP QUARTER-FINAL · 20 MARCH 2006

Recruited from Norwich City for a fee of £7.25M in January 2006, striker Dean Ashton paid a large chuck of that transfer fee back with both goals in the Hammers' 2-1 FA Cup quarter-final victory away to Manchester City.

Ashton had already impressed the West Ham faithful with three Premier League goals in his first six outings for the club and although he scored both goals in this Monday night match in Manchester, it was his first goal that gave the Hammers the lead four minutes before the break, that he is fondly remembered for.

A tight and close-fought affair was goalless as the highly-talented target-man won the ball and played a neat pass into midfield, before making a forward run and collecting the ball back just outside the City area. He then almost slalomed his way past two defenders before unleashing a ferocious shot that beat City 'keeper David James at his near post.

After the hosts had been reduced to ten men following the dismissal of Sun Jihai, eleven minutes into the second half, Ashton then netted his and the Hammers' second goal of the night after 69 minutes.

Kiki Musampa reduced the arrears five minutes from time to tee-up a nervy final five minutes, but the Hammers held firm as Ashton's brace set up a semi-final meeting with Middlesbrough.

8. PAOLO DI CANIO

WEST HAM UNITED 2
WIMBLEDON 0

PREMIER LEAGUE · 26 MARCH 2000

Paolo Di Canio's scissor-kick volley against Wimbledon was undoubtedly one of the most memorable goals scored at the Hammers' former home.

Such was the quality, the Italian's strike is still shown at the very top of any Premier League greatest goals montage, and rightly so. It was bold, it was brilliant, it was special, it was Paolo Di Canio summed up in one breathtaking, fluid movement.

Prior to the No 10's magic moment, the Hammers were enjoying an impressive, if not spectacular, Premier League season. Harry Redknapp's attractive and flamboyant side were certainly a force to be reckoned with on home turf, where they had won eight and lost just two of their 14 league matches prior to the Dons' visit. So it came as no surprise that West Ham took control of the game from the kick-off, ripping into their struggling opponents.

After only eight minutes, Sinclair crossed from the right and Di Canio, with both feet off the ground, volleyed home spectacularly with the outside of his right boot, past the despairing Sullivan. Simply sensational!

9. TONY COTTEE

WEST HAM UNITED 3-0 TOTTENHAM HOTSPUR

DIVISION ONE · 1 JANUARY 1983

It may have been a simple header from close-range with Spurs' goalkeeper Ray Clemence routed to the floor, but when Tony Cottee marked his Hammers debut with a goal a true West Ham United legend was born.

Born in Forest Gate and a lifelong Hammers fan, Cottee enjoyed a fairytale debut at Upton Park on New Year's Day 1983. Aged just 17, Cottee had been in fine form for the youth team the previous season and had already scored twelve goals in eight games for the reserves in 1982/83 before being handed his big chance in this First Division London derby match.

The goal was a perfect demonstration of Cottee's instinct and natural ability to put the ball in the back of the net. When Joe Gallagher's powerful header crashed against the Spurs crossbar, Cottee sprung into the air to plant the rebound into the net with the goalkeeper still squirming on the floor after his attempt to keep out Gallagher's initial header.

The goal won Cottee the headlines and plaudits and was the first of his 146 goal haul for the club across his two spells with his beloved Hammers.

10. RONNIE BOYCE

WEST HAM UNITED 3-2 PRESTON NORTH END
1964 FA CUP FINAL · 2 MAY 1964

For dramatic endings, there is unlikely to be anything in West Ham United history to top Ronnie Boyce's last-minute header that won the FA Cup for the Hammers in 1964.

Boyce's last-gasp goal put Ron Greenwood's side in front for the very first time in the match and with just a matter of seconds remaining there was no time for the North End to mount a comeback.

Boyce certainly was the toast of East London after his memorable header saw the FA Cup come to Upton Park for the first time in the club's history.

The late drama was a fitting end to what was a pulsating FA Cup Final. Throughout their run to the final, the Hammers showed great character and determination, and those qualities served the team superbly in the Wembley showpiece.

Preston opened the scoring after ten minutes through Doug Holden, but the Hammers' response was instant as John Sissons levelled just a minute later.

North End regained the lead five minute before the break with an Alex Dawson header. However, an inspired half-time team talk from Ron Greenwood saw the Hammers back on level terms just seven minutes into the second half.

Chances came and went for both teams until Boyce timed his run into the box to absolute perfection and he planted Peter Brabrook's right-wing cross past Alan Kelly for the winner.

TONY COTTEE

HAMMERS HERO

Born in Forest Gate on 11 July 1965, Tony Cottee began his career with West Ham United and went on to be became one of the most prolific and popular goalscorers in the club's history.

After proving to be a consistent goalscorer at both youth and reserve-team level, it was of little surprise that Cottee was handed his first-team debut at the age of just 17. Unsurprisingly, the striker marked the occasion with a goal as the Hammers registered a 3-0 New Year's Day victory over Spurs at the Boleyn Ground in 1983.

The 1983/84 campaign saw the striker really cement his place in the Hammers' starting line-up. Despite his tender years, he ended the season with 19 goals in all competitions - 15 in the First Division and four in the League Cup. His four League Cup goals all came in one game as the Hammers dished out a 10-0 thrashing to Bury at Upton Park. The match was equally as one-sided as this season's 8-0 victory against Macclesfield Town.

The following season, Cottee netted another 17 league goals and had amassed an impressive 37 top-flight goals by the age of 20.

During the 1985/86 season, as the Hammers stood toe-to-toe with Merseyside giants Liverpool and Everton in a three-way race for the title, manager John Lyall successfully paired Cottee with Frank McAvennie. Their partnership went on to yield an incredible 46 league goals as the Hammers ended a truly memorable campaign in third place - the club's best-ever top-flight finish.

McAvennie weighed in with 26 league goals while strike partner Cottee registered 20 and it was the local hero Cottee who won the 1986 Hammer of the Year accolade, with his sidekick as runner-up. Cottee's exploits in 1985/86 also saw him voted the PFA Young Player of the Year.

In the summer of 1988, Cottee briefly became the most expensive player to be signed by a British club when he joined Everton for £2.2M. The fee was eclipsed later that month when Merseyside rivals Liverpool resigned Ian Rush from Juventus.

After 72 goals from 184 league games for the Toffees, Cottee made a hero's return to Upton Park in September 1994. His first season back with the Hammers yielded 13 Premier League goals and helped ensure the club's top-flight status.

Across his two spells with the club, Cottee made a total of 336 appearances for the Hammers and scored 146 goals.

In October 1996, he joined Selangor of Malaysia and then returned to England with Leicester City in 1997, where he was a League Cup winner in 2000 under the management Martin O'Neill. He also played for Birmingham City on loan and briefly for Norwich City, before trying his luck in management with Barnet and ending his playing career at Millwall.

FULL NAME:	Antony Richard Cottee
DATE OF BIRTH:	11 July 1965
PLACE OF BIRTH:	Forest Gate, London
POSITION:	Striker

WHU APPEARANCES	WHU GOALS
336	**131**
LEAGUE: 279	LEAGUE: 115
FA CUP: 29	FA CUP: 12
LEAGUE CUP: 27	LEAGUE CUP: 18
OTHER: 1	OTHER: 1

DEBUT: **West Ham united 3-0 Spurs**
1 January 1983 · Division One

ENGLAND

APPEARANCES	GOALS
7	**0**

DEBUT: **Sweden 1-0 England**
10 September 1986

PREMIER LEAGUE 2

OLADAPO AFOLAYAN

POSITION: **Striker**   DOB: **12/02/98**

A quick, direct centre-forward with an eye for goal, Afolayan joined West Ham United from non-league club Solihull Moors on transfer deadline day in January 2018. The Harrow-born striker had previously attended Chelsea's Academy as a youngster.

TUNJI AKINOLA

POSITION: **Defender**   DOB: **21/11/98**

A defender with a promising future, Akinola began his Academy scholarship in 2015/16 and after playing regularly for the U18 side he progressed to feature for the development squad. He captained the U23 side for the first time last season and featured in the Checkatrade Trophy campaign.

JOSEPH ANANG

POSITION: Goalkeeper   **DOB:** 08/06/00

Ghanaian 'keeper Joseph Anang signed for the Hammers at scholar level having come over to England hoping to forge a career in the game. The stopper is a talented teenager who is known for his trademark side-on drop-kick, something that attracted the Hammers when signing him.

MARCUS BROWNE

POSITION: Midfielder   **DOB:** 18/12/97

Currently on loan with League One Oxford United, the attacking midfielder joined the Hammers' Academy at the age of eight. The direct forward-thinking player made his debut for West Ham as a substitute in the Europa League Play-Off draw at Astra Giurgiu in August 2016.

MASON BARRETT

POSITION: Defender   **DOB:** 24/09/99

Barrett is a versatile defender who has progressed through the various age groups within the Academy set-up at West Ham United. With the ability to operate anywhere across the back four, his flexibility has proved a great asset throughout his development.

CONOR COVENTRY

POSITION: Midfielder   **DOB:** 25/03/00

Midfielder Coventry began his scholarship with the Hammers in the summer of 2016. His form earned a call-up to the Republic of Ireland U17s where he became a regular for the Boys in Green. He made his first-team debut at London Stadium in the 8-0 victory over Macclesfield in the EFL Cup.

JAHMAL HECTOR-INGRAM

POSITION: Striker   **DOB:** 11/11/98

England youth international striker Hector-Ingram has been part of the West Ham United Academy since the age of six, and has long been thought of as a potential star of the future. Born and raised in Upton Park, he has been scoring goals at Academy level for a decade.

GRADY DIANGANA

POSITION: Midfielder   **DOB:** 19/03/98

Attacking midfielder Diangana continues to be an impressive performer for the U23 side, with the ability to operate in a variety of forward positions. He made his first-team debut at London Stadium in the 8-0 EFL Cup win over Macclesfield, scoring twice and earning him a Premier League debut as a late substitute three days later against Manchester United.

NATHAN HOLLAND

POSITION: Midfielder   **DOB:** 19/06/98

Manchester-born Holland joined West Ham in January 2017 from Everton and agreed a three-and-a-half-year deal at the club. His impressive performances since joining were rewarded with a first-team debut in the 3-0 EFL Cup victory over Bolton Wanderers in September 2017.

BEN JOHNSON

POSITION: **Midfielder**   DOB: **24/01/00**

A regular for the U18 and U23 sides over the past two seasons, Johnson has displayed his versatility by playing at right-back, right-midfield and in centre-midfield. The midfielder will be looking to cement his place in the U23 side in 2018/19.

ALFIE LEWIS

POSITION: **Midfielder**   DOB: **28/09/99**

An intelligent and highly-rated midfielder, Lewis boasts an impressing range of passing skills. He was a regular at U23 level last season, featuring in Premier League 2 and Checkatrade Trophy fixtures.

DAN KEMP

POSITION: **Midfielder**   DOB: **11/01/99**

Talented winger Kemp has made great progress with the Hammers and agreed a three-year professional contract in May 2016. He starred for the U23 side last season and grabbed the winner in the 3-2 Checkatrade Trophy win at Swindon Town in August 2017.

MOSES MAKASI

POSITION: **Midfielder**   DOB: **22/10/95**

Central midfielder Makasi is an Academy product who graduated in the summer of 2014 and established himself as a regular in the Development Squad and U23s. A leader on the pitch, Moses enjoyed a loan spell with League One Plymouth Argyle in the second-half of last season.

PL2

JOSH PASK

POSITION: Defender **DOB:** 01/11/97

Pask joined the Hammers' Academy at the age of eight and has progressed to become recognised as one of the most promising young central defenders at the club. He gained experience on loan to Dagenham and Redbridge in 2015 and spent the initial part of 2016/17 at Gillingham.

VASHON NEUFVILLE

POSITION: Defender **DOB:** 18/07/99

England U16 international defender Vashon Neufville joined West Ham United's Academy as an U14. He has progressed through the ranks and his performances have won him many admirers. The defender is now a regular at U23 level.

JOE POWELL

POSITION: Midfielder **DOB:** 30/10/98

A pacy wide man, Powell has produced a number of impressive displays while progressing though the Hammers' Academy. His U18 performances soon saw him playing regularly for the U23s and win a professional contract. He made his first-team debut in the 8-0 EFL Cup victory over Macclesfield.

ANTHONY SCULLY

POSITION: Midfielder   **DOB:** 03/12/99

An exciting talent who impressed throughout his two-year Academy scholarship, creative midfielder Scully signed his first professional contract at the end of the 2015/16 season. The midfielder has played internationally for the Republic of Ireland at U17 level.

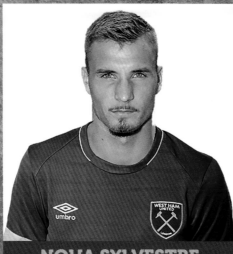

NOHA SYLVESTRE

POSITION: Midfielder   **DOB:** 29/12/97

A combative holding central midfielder, Sylvestre joined the Irons in 2014 from his native Switzerland after beginning his career with FC Bure. He has progressed via the U18 team and the development squad where his tough tackling and clever passing have won him many plaudits.

XANDE SILVA

POSITION: Striker   **DOB:** 16/03/97

Silva signed for West Ham's Academy in August 2018. The Portuguese forward had spent four years with Vitória Guimarães previously. He got his Hammers' career underway with a superb debut hat-trick against Spurs in the U23s' first PL2 match of the 2018/19 campaign.

NATHAN TROTT

POSITION: Goalkeeper   **DOB:** 21/11/98

Highly-rated Bermudan goalkeeper Trott joined West Ham United in January 2016 on a two-and-a-half-year deal following a successful trial period. The popular stopper has impressed at club level in 2017/18 and gained international recognition with England U20s.

SPOT THE SEASON

At the end of this historic campaign, West Ham United won promotion to the First Division for the first time in the club's history. They went into their last game of the season as league leaders, but were pipped to the Second Division title when they lost their final fixture 1-0 to eventual champions Notts County.

The campaign concluded with West Ham as runners-up with 51 league points and sealing the second promotion spot ahead of Leicester City on goal difference. Vic Watson ended the season as top scorer with 27 goals in all competitions, while inside-left Billy Moore was ever-present featuring in all 51 league and cup fixtures.

As well as winning promotion to the top-flight for the first time, West Ham United also featured in their first major cup final during this season. Under the management of Syd King the team were FA Cup finalists, but were beaten 2-0 by Bolton Wanderers in the Wembley final.

Can you spot the season?

2

West Ham really were the standout side in the Second Division this season as they won the title with a remarkable 13-point cushion from runners-up Notts County. Swansea City took the third and final promotion berth.

A memorable season also saw the team reach the League Cup Final where they drew 1-1 with Liverpool, thanks to a last-gasp penalty from Ray Stewart. Despite taking the lead in the replay at Villa Park, reigning First Division champions Liverpool recovered to win 2-1.

Goalkeeper Phil Parkes ended the season with the Hammer of the Year award, while David Cross top-scored with 33 goals in all competitions.

Can you spot the season?

John Lyall guided the Hammers back to the First Division in style as the Hammers secured the Second Division title at the end of this classic campaign.

3

After winning the FA Cup for the first time the previous season, West Ham United made their mark in European football defeating TSV Munich 1860 in the European Cup Winners' Cup Final during this mystery season.

Alan Sealey was the Hammers' Euro hero, netting both goals in the final at Wembley Stadium.

With Ron Greenwood as manager, the team enjoyed an impressive First Division campaign and ended the season in ninth place having amassed 42 points from their league programme. As FA Cup holders, the Hammers exited the competition at the fourth round stage after losing a London derby 1-0 at home to Chelsea.

Jonny Byrne was leading scorer with 30 goals in all competitions, 25 of his goals came in First Division fixtures, including a hat-trick against Spurs in a 3-2 triumph at Upton Park.

Can you spot the season?

SCOTT PARKER

HAMMERS HERO

Three-time Hammer of the Year Scott Parker was born in Lambeth on 13 October 1980. A Lilleshall graduate, Parker shot to fame as the 13-year-old keepie-uppie star of a McDonalds advert during the 1994 World Cup.

He began his professional career with Charlton Athletic, making his debut in 1997 and gaining useful first-team experience with a brief loan spell at Norwich City in 2000.

Parker, who was named as the PFA Young Player of the Year at the end of the 2003/04 season, had been consistently linked with moves away from Charlton. He finally left the Valley in January 2004 to join Chelsea on a four-and-a-half-year contract for a fee of £10M.

With first-team opportunities hard to come by at Stamford Bridge, Parker opted to move North to Newcastle United in July 2005 for £6.5m.

After six goals in 73 matches for the Magpies, the central midfielder with boundless energy, unrivalled commitment and inspirational leadership qualities, returned to the capital and was reunited with his former Charlton manager Alan Curbishley, when he joined the Hammers in the summer of 2007 for fee of £7M.

Over the next four outstanding seasons in East London, he produced arguably the best football of his illustrious career. Parker was voted Hammer of the Year for the first time in 2009, before winning the accolade again in 2010 and 2011, while his form also earned a recall to the senior England squad after a four-and-a-half year absence.

He played a total of 129 games for the Hammers, netting twelve goals. He joined London rivals Tottenham Hotspur in August 2011 following West Ham's relegation to the Championship. After two seasons at White Hart Lane, he joined Fulham in 2013.

Parker ended his playing days at Craven Cottage in 2017 hanging up his boots at the age of 36, calling time on a career that spanned 20 seasons, 572 senior games, 18 England caps and countless crunching tackles and lung-busting runs.

FULL NAME:	Scott Matthew Parker
DATE OF BIRTH:	13 October 1980
PLACE OF BIRTH:	Lambeth
POSITION:	Midfielder

WHU APPEARANCES	WHU GOALS
129	**12**
LEAGUE: 113	LEAGUE: 10
FA CUP: 6	FA CUP: 0
LEAGUE CUP: 10	LEAGUE CUP: 2

DEBUT:	**West Ham 1-0 Plymouth Argyle** 26 September 2007 · League Cup
HOTY:	**2008/09 · 2009/10 · 2010/11**

ENGLAND	
APPEARANCES	GOALS
18	**0**

DEBUT:	**England 2-3 Denmark** 16 November 2003

THE HAMMERS ACADEMY

Ajibola Alese

POSITION: Defender **DOB:** 17/01/01

Centre-back Ajibola Alese became a full-time scholar in summer 2017, by which time he had already made his U18 Premier League debut. At international level, he was capped three times at U16 level before graduating to the Young Lions' U17 squad.

Keenan Appiah-Forson

POSITION: Midfielder **DOB:** 16/10/01

A versatile first-year scholar, Appiah-Forson has featured in central midfield and at right-back and will be hoping to cement a place in the U18 team over the coming months.

Harrison Ashby

POSITION: Defender **DOB:** 14/11/01

A member of the U16 squad last season, defender Ashby can play as a centre-back or at right-back.

He stepped up to the U18s in 2017/18 and began his scholarship in July 2018.

Sean Adarkwa

POSITION: Striker **DOB:** 11/10/00

Versatile forward Adarkwa became a full-time scholar at the Hammers' Academy in July 2017. The teenager appeared 17 times in the U18 Premier League South as a first-year scholar in 2017/18, starting eleven games and twice.

Jamal Baptiste

POSITION: Defender **DOB:** 11/11/03

Schoolboy defender Baptiste is already a member of West Ham United's U18 squad. The defender scored in a pre-season victory over Colchester Utd in July before making his U18 Premier League South debut as a substitute in the opening day 4-1 win at Norwich City on 11 August.

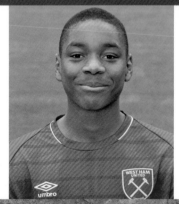

Kristijan Belic

POSITION: Midfielder **DOB:** 25/03/01

Serbian midfielder Kristijan Belic joined West Ham United as a 15-year-old before taking up a full-time scholarship in summer 2017. Born in Belgrade, Belic is a strong, committed and ball-winning player.

Jake Giddings

POSITION: Midfielder **DOB:** 07/11/01

Central midfielder Jake Giddings was another regular performer for the U16 side during the 2017/18 campaign. He will be looking to carry his good from into the new season as he begins his two-year scholarship.

Daniel Chesters

POSITION: Midfielder **DOB:** 01/04/02

Attacking midfielder Chesters is comfortable playing as a winger or in a more central role. He was a huge creative spark for the U16s in 2017/18 and stepped up to the U18s, before starting his scholarship ahead of 2018/19.

Will Greenidge

POSITION: Defender **DOB:** 15/05/02

Full-back Greenidge featured seven times in U18 Premier League South in 2017/18 while still a schoolboy, debuting at home to Southampton on 19 August 2017. He began his scholarship in summer 2018.

Kevin Dalipi

POSITION: Defender **DOB:** 22/01/01

Second-year scholar Dalipi will be looking to continue his development in 2018/19, the powerful defender was a regular in the U18 side last season during his first year as a full-time scholar.

Reece Hannam

POSITION: Defender **DOB:** 11/09/00

Left-back Hannam enjoyed an impressive first season as a full-time Hammers scholar in 2017/18. Such was his progress, that he stepped up to play for the U23 side and will be looking for more football at that level in 2018/19.

Anouar El Mhassani

POSITION: Midfielder **DOB:** 18/04/01

Exciting Dutch prospect El Mhassani joined the Hammers from Dutch giants Ajax in July 2018 after agreeing a three-year deal with the club. The left-footed 16-year-old can operate down either flank.

Daniel Jinadu

POSITION: Goalkeeper **DOB:** 21/06/02

Highly-rated 'keeper Jinadu was signed from Chelsea. The stopper has shared duties for England U16s with fellow Hammer Serine Sanneh. Jinadu was highly sought after and joined the Hammers following a successful trial period.

THE HAMMERS ACADEMY

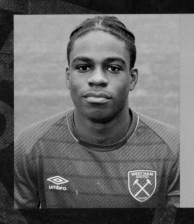

Jay Mingi

POSITION: Midfielder

DOB: 22/10/00

Mingi, a versatile midfielder who can also play in the centre of defence, has had a tough time with injuries this year, but is heading back to full fitness.

Sebastian Nebyla

POSITION: Midfielder **DOB:** 25/02/02

West Ham United secured the services of Slovakian defender Nebyla from Spartaka Trnava in May following the big defenders impressive displays for Trnava's youth sides. He began his scholarship with the Hammers in July 2018.

Emmanuel Longelo

POSITION: Forward **DOB:** 27/12/00

Exciting forward Longelo began his scholarship at the Hammers' Academy of Football in July 2017. With a season of full-time football under his belt, the youngster will be out to impress at both U18 and U23 level in 2018/19.

Jeremy Ngakia

POSITION: Midfielder

DOB: 07/09/00

Flying winger Ngakia loves to use his pace and power on the right-hand-side, and can also fill in at full-back.

Kyle McGeachy

POSITION: Defender

DOB: 30/03/01

Defender Kyle McGeachy has broken into the U18s this season and started the side's first game this campaign against Norwich City.

Sam Nsumbu

POSITION: Defender **DOB:** 30/04/02

Nsumbu is one of nine players from the Hammers' Academy U16 squad to have been offered a scholarship ahead of the 2018/19 campaign. He was a regular face in the U16s side last season.

Josh Okotcha

POSITION: Defender **DOB:** 19/12/01

Central defender Okotcha tasted U18 Premier League football while still plying his trade for the U16s. That experience is sure to serve him well having now begun his two-year scholarship with the Hammers.

Serine Sanneh

POSITION: Goalkeeper **DOB:** 20/11/02

Hammers' U15 goalkeeper during 2017/18, Sanneh's performances have won him international recognition with England at U16 level. He made his U18s debut against Leicester City in February 2018.

Veron Parkes

POSITION: Midfielder **DOB:** 28/09/01

First-year scholar Parkes, is a highly-rated youngster who joined from Crystal Palace. The pacy, technically-skilled attacking player, capable of playing as a winger or an attacking midfielder, featured for the U16s and U18s in 2017/18.

Odysseas Spyrides

POSITION: Midfielder

DOB: 17/01/01

Cypriot attacker Spyrides is aiming to sign his first professional contract at the end of what he hopes will be a successful season in the U18s.

Lennon Peake

POSITION: Midfielder **DOB:** 22/07/02

Skilful winger Peake joined eight of his U16 teammates from 2017/18 by starting a two-year scholarship at West Ham United's Academy of Football in the summer of 2018.

Peter Stroud

POSITION: Midfielder **DOB:** 23/04/02

USA U17 international midfielder Stroud joined the Hammers from the New York Red Bulls Academy.

He began his scholarship at the West Ham Academy in July 2018.

Bernardo Rosa

POSITION: Midfielder

DOB: 20/09/00

An U18 playing up in the U23s, creative Brazilian Rosa has been terrific this campaign and has plenty of potential.

Louie Watson

POSITION: Midfielder **DOB:** 06/07/01

A regular in the Hammers' U18 side last season, talented midfielder Watson has been capped by England at youth level having represented the Three Lions' sides at U15 and U16 level.

FAST FORWARD>>

Do your predictions for 2018/19 match our own?…

PREMIER LEAGUE WINNERS
Liverpool

PREMIER LEAGUE TOP SCORER
Sergio Agüero

PREMIER LEAGUE RUNNERS-UP
Manchester City

RELEGATED TO THE CHAMPIONSHIP: 18TH
Southampton

RELEGATED TO THE CHAMPIONSHIP: 19TH
Fulham

BOTTOM OF THE PREMIER LEAGUE
Newcastle United

FA CUP WINNERS
West Ham United

FA CUP RUNNERS-UP
Manchester United

LEAGUE CUP WINNERS
Arsenal

LEAGUE CUP RUNNERS-UP
Leicester City

CHAMPIONSHIP WINNERS

Leeds United

CHAMPIONSHIP RUNNERS-UP

Middlesbrough

CHAMPIONSHIP PLAY-OFF WINNERS

Derby County

CHAMPIONSHIP TOP SCORER

Neal Maupay

Brentford

HAMMERS' TOP SCORER

Marko Arnautović

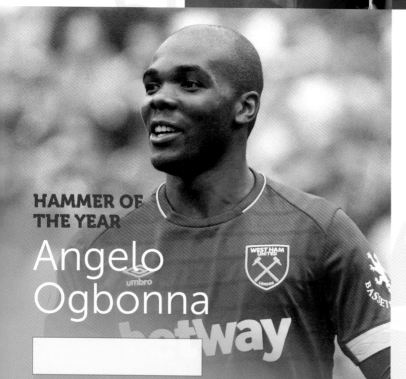

HAMMER OF THE YEAR

Angelo Ogbonna

CHAMPIONS LEAGUE WINNERS

Juventus

CHAMPIONS LEAGUE RUNNERS-UP

Barcelona

EUROPA LEAGUE WINNERS

Arsenal

EUROPA LEAGUE RUNNERS-UP

AC Milan

77

WHU WOMEN

4. Brooke Hendrix

POSITION: Defender **DOB:** 06/05/93

American defender Hendrix signed for the Hammers in the summer of 2018. The vastly-experienced 6'0 centre-half has played for Rangers, Swiss Nationalliga A side FC Staad, Icelandic outfit Fylkir and Italian club Brescia.

5. Gilly Flaherty

POSITION: Defender **DOB:** 24/08/91

An England international, Flaherty joined West Ham United Women on the back of four years with Chelsea Women, during which the centre-back secured two FA Women's Super League championships and two Women's FA Cup triumphs.

1. Becky Spencer

POSITION: Goalkeeper **DOB:** 22/02/91

Becky joined West Ham United Women from Chelsea in the summer of 2018. Spencer moved to the Irons after two years with the Blues, having enjoyed a career which has also seen her play for Arsenal, ASJ Soyaux, and Birmingham City.

6. Tessel Middag

POSITION: Midfielder **DOB:** 23/12/92

Middag joined from Manchester City in 2018, having spent two years at City. She made her international debut for the Netherlands back in 2012, featuring against France, and has now played over 40 times for her nation, scoring four goals.

2. Ria Percival

POSITION: Defender **DOB:** 07/12/89

Born in Essex, Percival played in her home nation New Zealand with Lynn-Avon United until 2008, before moving to United American Soccer League team F.C. Indiana. The right-back, who can also play further up field has over 100 caps for New Zealand.

7. Alisha Lehmann

POSITION: Forward **DOB:** 21/01/99

Lehmann signed for West Ham in the summer of 2018 from Swiss team BSC Young Boys Frauen. The 19-year-old has also made an impact at international level in her short career, making her full debut for the Swiss team in 2017.

3. Erin Simon

POSITION: Defender **DOB:** 19/08/94

Simon joined West Ham on a free transfer, having left American side Sky Blue FC at the end of 2017/18. Versatile in the back line, Erin began her college football career with Syracuse Orange in New York.

8. Leanne Kiernan

POSITION: Striker **DOB:** 27/04/99

Kiernan excelled at cross country and Gaelic football as a schoolgirl and at 15 joined Shelbourne Ladies. Her goals helped Shelbourne win the National League title, while her hat-trick secured the FAI Cup. She joined the Hammers in July 2018.

9. Jane Ross

POSITION: Forward   **DOB:** 18/09/89

Ross started her career in Scotland with Glasgow City, where she won six Scottish Women's Premier League titles, three Scottish cups and three League Cups. She joined the Hammers from Manchester City in the summer of 2018.

10. Julia Simic

POSITION: Midfielder   **DOB:** 14/05/89

Simic moved to West Ham United in the summer of 2018. An experienced international, she made her senior debut against Austria in 2016 and was part of the Germany squad that won the UEFA Women's U19 Championship in 2007.

11. Claire Rafferty

POSITION: Defender   **DOB:** 11/01/89

England international Rafferty signed for West Ham Women in 2018 after eleven seasons with Chelsea. She played a crucial role for the Blues' side that claimed the FA WSL title and FA Women's Cup on two occasions - both double-winning seasons.

12. Kate Longhurst

POSITION: Midfielder   **DOB:** 20/05/89

Lifelong Hammers fan Longhurst moved to West Ham in 2018 after a five-year stint with Liverpool, where she played Champions League football. Born in Witham, Kate initially made the move into football as a youngster with Colchester.

13. Anna Moorhouse

POSITION: Goalkeeper   **DOB:** 30/03/95

Moorhouse joined from Arsenal in the summer of 2018, after spending the 2017 Spring Series and 2017/18 with the Gunners. Originally starting her professional career with Everton Ladies, Anna has also played for Durham and Doncaster Rovers Belles.

14. Vyan Sampson

POSITION: Defender   **DOB:** 02/07/96

Sampson signed her West Ham deal after seven years with Arsenal, having made three appearances for the Hammers at the end of 2017/18 in the Premier League Southern Division. She has also been capped for England at U19 and U17 level.

15. Brianna Visalli

POSITION: Midfielder   **DOB:** 17/4/95

Visalli signed from Chicago Red Stars in the summer of 2018. An impressive season in her final year of eligibility for draft with Pepperdine University, in which she scored 14 goals and provided six assists, saw Brianna picked by Chicago during the 2018 NWSL College Draft.

16. Rosie Kmita

POSITION: Forward   **DOB:** 27/07/94

Attacker Kmita joined West Ham Women from WSL2 side London Bees in October 2017. She spent her formative years with Tottenham Hotspur Ladies before joining Brighton & Hove Albion at the age of 18.

17. Esmee De Graaf

POSITION: Striker   **DOB:** 02/08/97

De Graaf joined West Ham from PEC Zwolle where she enjoyed a three-year spell, during which she broke into the Netherlands international side. She has played twice for her country and was part of the squad that lifted the Algarve Cup.

18. Lucienne Reichardt

POSITION: Midfielder   **DOB:** 01/05/92

Reichardt moved to east London from Ajax, after two years with the current Eredivisie Vrouwen champions. She won seven trophies during her time in Holland and will be looking to continue her trophy success with West Ham Women.

THE MOMENT

Hammers legend Trevor Brooking stooped to head the Wembley winner that brought the FA Cup back to the Boleyn

FIXTURE:	1980 FA Cup Final
DATE:	Saturday 10 May 1980
SCORE:	West Ham United 1-0 Arsenal
VENUE:	Wembley
ATTENDANCE:	100,000

Against all the odds West Ham United defied their underdogs tag to win the 1980 FA Cup on a truly memorable occasion for all Irons fans.

London rivals Arsenal provided the opposition, but with the Hammers then a Second Division club, there were not too many people outside of Upton Park who were predicting anything more than a routine victory for First Division Gunners.

Arsenal enjoyed a majority of the possession in the opening ten-minute period, but it was the Hammers who shocked the nation by opening the scoring with their first meaningful move forward.

Winger Alan Devonshire broke away down the left flank and cleverly worked his way to the line before sending in a deep teasing cross that fell to striker David Cross whose effort on goal was blocked by defender Willie Young. Stuart Pearson then sent Young's clearance back across the face of the Gunners' goal where Trevor Brooking stooped swiftly inside the six yard box to send a flicked header past Pat Jennings in the Arsenal goal.

A goal to the good after 13 minutes, John Lyall's side stood toe-to-toe with Arsenal for the remainder of the first half and fully deserved their goal advantage at the break.

The second-half saw the Gunners search desperately for an equaliser, but despite good spells of possession, they just could not find a way past Hammers' keeper Phil Parkes and the resolute defence that stood in front of him.

The Hammers almost added to their lead in the closing stages when Paul Allen broke free and closed in, one-on-one with Jennings. Just as Allen looked set to strike into the penalty area, the youngster was cynically fouled by defender Young. Prior to the days of the professional foul rule, the Arsenal man escaped with a yellow card.

Despite their possession, Arsenal failed to break West Ham down and when referee George Courtney blew the final whistle, it sent the whole of East London delirious.

As Bonds collected the trophy from the Duchess of Kent and raised it above his head toward the jubilant Hammers' supporters, a chorus of cheers and "I'm Forever Blowing Bubbles", echoed around Wembley stadium.

The victory was the Hammers' third FA Cup triumph following the previous successes of 1964 and 1975. It was also the last time a side from outside the top-flight has lifted the famous trophy.